SEEDS FROM THE ASHES
A New Way to Think and Live

Seeds from the Ashes

SEEDS FROM THE ASHES
A New Way to Think and Live

MALCOLM KELLY

BYE PUBLISHING

OAKLAND, SACRAMENTO, CALIFORNIA

Seeds from the Ashes

Seeds from the Ashes

Copyright @ 2010 by Malcolm Kelly
All rights reserved. No part of this book may be used or reproduced in any manner whatsoever without written permission from the publisher, except in brief quotations embodied in articles and reviews.

For information address:
BYE Publishing Services
5245 College Avenue, Suite 333
Oakland, CA 94618
510-272-0101

Web site: www.byepublishing.com

Library of Congress Control Number: 2006904510

ISBN: 0-9656739-6-0
ISBN: 978-0-9656739-6-9

A SELF-EMPOWERMENT BOOK
Printed in the United States of America
First Printing: 2010

DEDICATION

I dedicate this book to all those individuals who are searching for ways to change their lives. I trust they will find it to be a valuable tool to assist them with the challenges they face on their arduous journeys of self-discovery and freedom.

Seeds from the Ashes

ACKNOWLEDGMENTS

I am deeply grateful to my wife, Carolyn, for her encouragement and support during the early stages of the book. After so many years, she remains committed to my work.

I salute and thank the members of the National BYE Society for providing me with a forum to develop my ideas. Many of them did so without realizing they were not only receiving information, but giving it, too.

Seeds from the Ashes

CONTENTS

Introduction

Chapter One	Clearing the Mind to Think	25
Chapter Two	Self-Discovery	35
Chapter Three	The Higher Self	59
Chapter Four	Love	69
Chapter Five	Peace	87
Chapter Six	Wisdom	101
Chapter Seven	Freedom	113
Chapter Eight	Abundance	133
Chapter Nine	Power	147
Chapter Ten	Creation	161
Chapter Eleven	Vision of a New Person	179
Chapter Twelve	Confirm your Training	193
Chapter Thirteen	Vision of a New Family	207

Seeds from the Ashes

Introduction

I am writing *Seeds from the Ashes* specifically for those individuals whose beliefs have been shaped by the cultural ideas of victim consciousness. Most victims in this country are affected philosophically and culturally by the ideas and beliefs created and nurtured by generations of individuals who believed they were powerless to change their lives without assistance from someone else.

This book describes how you can use your mind to create other options for living that will assist you with changing the way you think and live. It is a blueprint for empowering individuals to overcome their obstacles by discovering how to use their inner-mind power to change their lives. When someone who has been deprived of power for so long is introduced to power, it is difficult for them to believe they have this type of power available to them.

They see life only from the prism of a victim.

The goal of the book is to inform those in positions of power in this country that because someone lives as a victim, that doesn't make them powerless to change the way they think and live. All the programs in the world cannot change the cultural decadence caused by generations of socially conditioned people who have been taught to rely on the government or God to solve their problems.

The society creates victims who seek to escape from its power by trying to assimilate into a white American culture. It doesn't matter how many victims physically leave the ghetto, they still continue to live with some of the victim beliefs. Even when victims achieve status in government, the media, sports, and so forth, they continue to think and live as victims. If you watch closely, you will hear and see in their voices and demeanor the anger, frustration, and self-hatred caused by oppressive racial experiences.

For many victims, living in this country is an unrelenting nightmare. In this nightmare, they must learn how to live with less and daydream about having more. After awhile, some of the more frustrated ones will seek to oppress other victims who are too weak and too afraid to challenge them. Society brands this type of behavior as "Black-on-Black crime," or "Hispanic-on-Hispanic crime." Unfortunately, it is probably best described as victims fighting victims over control of the ghetto.

Introduction

Seeds from the Ashes is a step-by-step process for America's victims to learn how to recognize and change self-destructive behavior. It is a book for anyone who desires to know how to take the first step to change their life. It is different from your typical book because you don't have to read it from cover to cover to enjoy its essence. It is a workshop-driven book with lots of ideas and suggestions about how to take that first step to change your life.

Today, after months, perhaps years, of feeling trapped in the miasma of failure and discontentment, you are finally able to do something about it. That's how I felt when I began writing this book. I wanted someone to help me to help myself. The illusions of lack, limitation, struggle, and doubt had overwhelmed me to the point where I felt powerless to solve my problems.

If this type of thinking seems strange to hear from someone who teaches empowerment to others, you are correct, it is. It's not only strange, but it's also somewhat disturbing to find yourself in such a lowly state of mind. Yet anyone who works on himself or herself over a long period of time seems to inevitably ask: How did I end up in this position?

For you to go beyond the problems in your life, you must overcome the bad—bad in the sense of deleterious—habits causing you all the pain. These illusive critters scurry about in your mind like bugs, hiding and eating whatever they can. Since they live in your thought patterns, it's very difficult to know which ones are harmful and which ones are harmless. This means you must examine each one to discover whether they are harmless or not.

When you begin your search to find the destructive habits shaping your thought patterns, you must realize that you are searching for some cold-blooded killers. These killer-thoughts wait patiently for you to ignore them and then without any warning, they quickly choke the life out of your desires. When they destroy thousands of your desires, you will have no choice but to hunt them down and destroy them all before they destroy you.

The sparks of change ignited in your mind come from the burning desire to reclaim your life. Your illumined thoughts become the light you need to create a clear vision of what you want to accomplish with your life. The vision is the light that will guide you in your search to find and destroy your harmful habits. It is important to know that your vision must be created from clear thoughts. If not, you cannot see clearly where you are going. A clear vision sees all obstacles.

The vision to change how you think and live is available to anyone who perceives himself or herself as weak, powerless, and a victim. Unfortunately, many individuals don't recognize they are victims until they reach very low points of emotional pain and suffering. When you hit the emotional bottom of your life, you are ready to change. This feeling might last for only a few hours or days, so it's important to take action immediately to overcome the problems causing you the pain and suffering. This means you must search for the not-so-obvious methods—those that exist within you—to change the way you think and live.

The empowerment tools in this book discuss those not-so-obvious ways to change the way you think and live. They address the emotional pain you feel when you reach the lowest point in your life, a place where you feel there's nowhere to go.

One of the primary reasons for writing this book is to share some empowerment tools with those who desire to change their lives and those who have become dependent on outside sources such as self-help books, seminars, audiotapes, and motivational speakers. It is also for those who find themselves stuck neatly into meaningless careers and relationships.

While this book is labeled a self-help book, it distinguishes itself from traditional books by focusing on taking the first step in the change-your-life process. This first step is very important, because most people don't know what to do to change their lives. How do you get started? After you think about it for awhile, you quickly realize the importance of the first step.

The ideas and suggestions in the book are to enlighten and to comfort you on the long, arduous journey to overcome the habits that are causing you so much pain and emotional suffering. By enlightening your mind to see that all power is in your mind, you acknowledge that the Creator (your higher consciousness) speaks to you with the same clarity as was spoken to the enlightened ones thousands of years ago.

Today, there are many who believe that certain people are victims in life because of their race and skin color. These same individuals generally agree that most victims in this country are African Americans, Latin Americans, and Native Americans. The sociological studies about education, wealth, and status all confirm this viewpoint. These same studies also cry loudly for someone to do something about this blight on a great society. This book is a step in that direction.

One of the troubling questions I had to confront before I began writing this book was: Who is responsible for changing the way someone thinks, acts, works, and lives? I also thought about the effects that racism and its corollary problems of illiteracy, poverty, cultural decay, and political impotency have had on conditioning the minds of so many people to believe they are powerless to change the way they think and live. It didn't take long for me to realize that each individual, regardless of his or her state of affairs, is responsible for changing the way he or she thinks and lives.

Nevertheless, as I write now, my thoughts are flashing with electrifying visions of inner-city families whose sons and daughters are in prison, those whose children have been murdered by guns, drugs, and alcohol, and those who have little or no formal education, suffer from chronic unemployment and underemployment, and live on the mercy of some government organization while praying for God to rescue them from the wretchedness associated with living in a society that looks unfavorably upon them. For some reason,

I can't get these people out of my mind. Perhaps it is because at one time I was one of them.

While I wrote the book primarily to address the problems faced by African, Latin, and Native American victims in this society, I also knew that I was I writing it for Europeans, Asians, Indians, Arabs, and all other groups of people striving to change their lives. The power to change the way you think and live transcends the limitations of skin color and race. This power can be expressed by anyone who desires to overcome his or her limitations.

When you think of yourself as black, white, brown, or yellow, you accept the ideas associated with these skin colors. So, if your skin color happens to be black, you probably accept that you are of African descent, which labels you an African American or black. By accepting societal labels to identify who you are, you learn how to live as a victim in this country. And as a victim, you learn how to ascribe blame to others— parents, God, teachers, neighborhood, police, whites, and so forth—for the way you live. Each day you relive the experience of being black and oppressed by all the forces of power in your life. It might appear to you that everyone oppressing you has power and you can't do anything about it. Overcome with victim beliefs, you condition your powerful mind to abdicate its power to a weak, victimized body with no sense of ever achieving power.

After you live this way for a number of years, it is easy for you to believe that *real* power exists only outside of you. Whenever someone tells you that you have the power to overcome the obstacles in your life, you find this difficult to accept. You ask yourself, "How can I have power and live the way I am living?" So you begin to search for power from sources outside of yourself, because no one has conditioned you to believe you have the power to change your own life.

Most victim-thinking individuals born and raised in America's ghettos believe their living conditions are so terrible that they try to destroy everything around them. For them, desirable neighborhoods are those places where there are few reminders of the ghetto. This type of thinking confirms the victim's beliefs about living with less while daydreaming about having more.

The empowerment tools in the book are to assist you with moving beyond daydreaming to problem solving. This process teaches you how to create a real-life vision of empowerment: a vision of yourself with the power to change how you think and live.

The ideas and techniques for creating a vision of empowerment are not a magical formula that will change your life in a few seconds, a few days, or even a few months. They are tools for you to use to guide you through a workable step-by-step process that will assist you with living a more purpose-fulfilled life.

One of the tools is the use of the seven lights of empowerment to illustrate your higher consciousness and give substance to your thoughts. This process allows you to define the power you use to create a new way to think and live.

To help define the seven lights of empowerment—*love, peace, wisdom, freedom, abundance, power*, and *creation*—I have employed a method of writing to describe the process someone uses to listen to the silent voices within his or her higher consciousness, which I describe as the intuitive consciousness. It is my intent for the reader to understand that the dialogue you have with yourself is analogous to the type of dialogue you have when you believe the Creator or the voice within you is speaking to you. The characters and mind-expansion exercises are merely reflections of your thoughts.

Another way to view the dialogue is to compare it to some of the writings used to tell stories in the Bible. For example, the story of Daniel being in the lions' den is not a literal story of him being surrounded by hungry lions. It is a story to tell you about what happens when you maintain your commitment to your vision of empowerment when you are faced with impending danger. The lions are metaphors for lack, limitation, struggle, and powerlessness, the enemies of success and empowerment.

Most people, unlike Daniel, are so mesmerized by their debts, failed relationships, chemical addictions, unemployment, and hopelessness that they end up being overcome or eaten by their problems. Instead of turning from the lions to look to the Creator (higher consciousness) as Daniel did, they focus only on the impending problems.

The problems you face now are similar to those Daniel faced in the lions' den. Now, can you, like Daniel did, take your attention away from your problems and focus only on expressing your vision of empowerment? If you can do this now, you will, like Daniel, not be harmed, but rescued.

The seven lights of empowerment express themselves as examples in the lives of Native Americans, Africans, Jews, British, Greeks, Chinese, Indians, and Arabs. These examples are mind-expansion exercises to remind you that all people have the power to change the way they think and live. They also motivate you to think creatively about using your power to solve your current problems.

To further assist you with your creative explorations, an anecdote is used to describe a real-life experience for each of the seven lights of empowerment. The anecdote is followed by a review of the material and how to relate it to your own experiences. After each review, there are suggestions to assist you with your daily activities to achieve empowerment.

The seven lights of empowerment are a part of all of us. They remind you of the potential you have to be so much greater than you are currently aware of being. This is particularly true for those who find themselves today mired deep in problems of depression, anger, self-hatred, lack, limitation and doubt. When you feel overwhelmed with problems, it is difficult to believe you are a powerful person who can solve all your problems. Yet this is what you must think of yourself if you truly want to change the way you think and live.

To solve your emotional and psychological problems, you have to go beyond the boundaries and labels that define you as a victim. For someone burdened with victim beliefs, it is a major breakthrough in self-development just to think of yourself as having great power.

When I first began to write about the seven lights of empowerment, I asked myself: Does anyone really care about something so abstract? Then I realized that the abstract, the intangible, is what change is all about: the ability to think of something existing that is not yet present in the world.

Even though the seven lights of empowerment are part of my writer's imagination, things I use to describe my ideas, I feel a kinship with them. During the course of clarifying my ideas, I constantly wondered whether my thoughts were actually the thoughts of the Creator (my higher consciousness) or those of a confused, delusional man. Did the Creator really talk to me with the same clarity and love that was spoken to Moses, Jesus, Mohammed, Siddhartha Gautama, the spiritual writers of the Synoptic Gospels of the Bible, the writers of the beautiful spiritual prose of the Koran, the Bhagavad-Gita, the Upanishads, and the Dead Sea Scrolls? I told myself yes, because we all were created by the same power.

At each level, each step on the journey, I use this form of

communicating to explain how other humans of different races and countries have risen to higher levels of awareness. And by doing so, they become examples of how you, too, can rise to these levels and even higher levels.

Contemporary clichés about inner power and the ability of someone to talk directly to the Creator are usually nothing but vain attempts to convince others of your greatness; a greatness that you know doesn't exist in your life. For many people, this failure to embody and express power in their lives becomes a stumbling block to changing the way they think about themselves. Fortunately, it is not fatal, because you can do something about it.

When you search for solutions to your problems, you will come face to face with the seven lights of empowerment. The virtues found in the lights are the ones you need to change the way you think and live. They are not something you can actually teach someone else. You can tell others about what they mean, but they have to search for them beyond their own intellectualism and emotional hang-ups. It is there, beyond the limitations of success and failure, where you will discover the secrets of the seven lights of empowerment.

There are many teachers who can write about and teach others about empowerment without themselves being empowered. These individuals are usually intellectually empowered, but they are still victims of the illusions.

For many victims, the ability to overcome a problem is

sometimes clouded within the joy of having done so. This joy, if left unchecked, can easily turn into egoism. And when it does, you become a victim of misguided information about yourself and the power you have to overcome a problem. Anyone can overcome a problem if they believe they have the right tools. For example, if you have an alcohol or drug problem, you need the right tools (resources) to overcome the problem. If you have them, then you will be successful; if not, you will continue to suffer with the addiction.

What are the right tools for you to use to solve your problems? I know the answers are within you; however, you might believe the answers are found somewhere else. And that's okay. The point here is that you are seeking answers to your problems. And if you look deep within your mind, you will discover the tools you need to change the way you think and live.

Seeds from the Ashes

Chapter One

Clearing the Mind to Think

The ability to change is a God-given power.
Are you the person that you want to be? There is nothing magical about changing your life. You don't need college degrees, great wealth, a deep religious faith, or public approval. You need only a strong, untainted desire to achieve success in your life. This desire will shape your vision for achieving success. It will confirm that you are endowed with the power to change your life. Yes, this simple desire in your head is what all great people have used to achieve their greatness. Now it is your turn to use this power for yourself.

How do you feel inside when you think of yourself as great and successful? Unworthy? Doubtful? Embarrassed? Whatever you feel in this moment will affect the potency of your desire. If your desire is encumbered by unworthiness, doubtfulness, or shamefulness, then your vision will contain these feelings. That is why it is so important to devote significant time to cleansing your thoughts. As you work on cleansing and transcending those thoughts causing you to doubt yourself, you will realize that change takes time, but it is attainable.

Every decision you ever made in your life had the power to create pain and suffering, wealth or poverty, or happiness and freedom. Most of us believe none of the decisions we ever made was intended to cause us pain and suffering. We tend to expect everything we do to produce success and prosperity. However, when we don't see these results, we begin to create little pockets of doubt about our powers to succeed in life.

The self-doubts in your life today represent all the things—beliefs about yourself and your position in the world—that you have acquired up to this point in your life. The measure of your success and failure in life is manifested within your thoughts about where you are today. If you don't like what you have produced in life, you have the power to change your life by producing something different. If you do like what you have produced in life, then you may not have an intense desire to make a commitment to change your life.

The difficulties you face today are the ones all of us face whenever we desire to change our lives. We begin to listen to those silent, inner thoughts. Those thoughts define your spiritual uniqueness in the manner that your DNA defines your human uniqueness. While most people devote years to learning about their human uniqueness, very few are willing to devote a lifetime to searching for answers about how their silent, inner thoughts hold the key to their spiritual uniqueness.

When you discuss your inner thoughts with other people, they listen but most fail to understand what you hear and see. They know only what they hear and see, not what you hear and see. The truth about you and your uniqueness is contained in your inner thoughts, not someone else's. Yes, you are human, but your spiritual thoughts distinguish you from all other humans. So what works for you might not work for me or someone else. Your desire to change is not connected to someone else's desire to change.

Clearing the mind of the illusionary weeds of self-destruction.

The inner voices you hear today, prodding you to continue reading this book, are present because of your desire to acquire new beliefs that will change your life. These voices have always been a part of your consciousness. However, until today, they were unnoticed thoughts, the type you ignore or accept as routine. When you decide to change, you want everything and everybody to recognize the urgency of your decision. You want to change right now. Regardless of how many times you hear or read that change is a slow process, you still want something to happen quickly. This feeling of urgency is similar to you expecting an immediate cure from medication prescribed by a doctor to treat a painful injury. For the medicine to work successful, you must be committed to taking it everyday.

The moment you stop and listen to the inner voices within you is the moment you seriously examine your life. After you decide to examine your life, you quickly discover how you have messed it up. You are shocked, dumbstruck by the density of the illusions growing wildly in your consciousness. There are illusions present everywhere you turn. These illusions, dominated by lack, limitation, and struggle, are the culprits responsible for the pain you feel right now. They keep you locked in spiritual complacency, unable to develop new ideas to change your life.

Sometime the weeds of your illusions overwhelm you to the point that you believe you can never get rid of all of them. Most people in this situation seek to hire a gardener—Jesus, Mohammed, Buddha, or a minister—to tend their garden. In other words, they turn over the illusions (problems) to someone else. This psychological transfer of power allows you to believe that something is happening magically in your life without you doing the work to solve your own problems.

After you have transferred your problems to someone else, you cheerfully tell anyone who will listen that you have been "saved" from the destruction of the illusions. The illusions can no longer cause pain and suffering in your life. You cheerfully tell folks that yesterday you were weak, but today you are strong. Furthermore,

Clearing the Mind to Think

this miraculous transformation occurred the moment you turned your life over to someone else.

Today, you realize that you are the gardener who must remove the illusions from your garden (consciousness). You must face the seemingly daunting task of removing thousands of illusions from your consciousness. You must do the work even when you don't feel like doing it. There are days when you feel like giving up, too tired to continue. There are other days when you feel like everything is going great. Then, there are those days when you would like to change how you are living, but you just can't seem to do it.

Well, the first step is to envision yourself looking and acting differently from the way you have in the past. Some people wonder what it means to envision yourself as a different person. How do you do something like this when your life is in such despair and chaos? How do you change when you are afraid to? Who helps you to change?

1. HOW DO YOU ENVISION YOURSELF WITH THE POWER TO CHANGE YOUR LIFE?
2. HOW DO YOU KNOW THAT TRUSTING YOUR INNER THOUGHTS WILL WORK?
3. HOW DO YOU CHANGE YOUR LIFE WHEN YOU FEEL POWERLESS TO DO SO?
4. HOW LONG DOES IT TAKE TO CHANGE YOUR LIFE?

ENVISION YOURSELF WITH THE POWER TO CHANGE YOUR LIFE

1. Sit down in a comfortable seat, somewhere alone, away from other people. I suggest you create a place in your home for you to meditate.
2. Take several deep breaths and slowly close your eyes. This will allow you to shut the door to your senses, which confirm the lack in your life, and open a new door to your inner-intuitive thoughts.
3. With your eyes closed, imagine your thoughts with the power to produce actions.
4. Use your thoughts to clearly see each weed (problem) existing in your garden of success and prosperity. Identify those weeds that need to be removed immediately. Spell out each problem with your thoughts and write them down on an imaginary piece of paper. See the debts, unemployment, fears, worries, self-doubts, addictions, failures, and powerlessness as words on that imaginary piece of paper.
5. Next imagine yourself as a colorless, formless, and faceless being with the power to create different realities in your life. Use this power to command your thoughts to become active with the energy to travel effortlessly within the boundless space of your mind.
6. Now, slowly command your thoughts to travel away from

your victim consciousness of lack, limitation, and struggle into a new time continuum where you are free of all problems.
7. From this new time continuum that includes past, present, and future time references, see how your life has evolved from past actions to the present moment.
8. While you are in the present moment, see yourself living with power, freedom, abundance, creation, wisdom, love, and peace.
9. From this place in your consciousness, there are no doubts about your power to express many different realities in your life.
10. Now, take a deep breath and exhale while saying "I am successful. I am empowered."

ACTIONS TO CHANGE YOUR LIFE WHEN YOU FEEL POWERLESS TO DO SO

There is a hollow feeling, an emptiness of purpose, in your mind when you feel powerless to change the way you think and live. Most people feel this way all the time. They feel trapped in unhappy marriages, dead-end jobs, cramped apartments, mortgaged homes, burgeoning debts, and burning desires for money, power, and fame. Perhaps you feel this way today.

Whenever you feel powerless to do something that you want to do, stop and ask yourself why. Why don't you have the power to achieve the things that you desire to have? The obvious answer is that you don't believe you are strong enough to achieve them. If this is the case, then the solution to your problem is attaining the necessary strength or power to solve your problem.

How do you attain this power? You attain power the same way as you attain anything else: you work for it. The harder you work, the greater your reward. If you desire to have a well-conditioned body, you must exercise regularly and monitor what you eat. If you desire to have a well-conditioned mind, you must exercise it regularly and monitor what you allow to enter into it.

Some people have the resources to hire personal trainers to assist them with their conditioning program, while many others without such resources, either do it themselves or postpone action until they get the resources. For you to begin to acquire the power you need to change your life, your exercise program must begin now with you acting as your own personal trainer.

As a trainer, you assume expert status as someone who is eminently qualified to guide you during your mind-conditioning training. This type of thinking requires you to assume two roles: first, as someone who knows what you need, and second, as someone who is willing to listen. The two roles occur within your mind as your intuitive consciousness and your victim consciousness. The former is free of the illusions that victimize the latter.

The similarities between power and powerless are present in all of your activities. Unfortunately, those who think of themselves as victims seldom recognize the distinctions between the two. It is this lack of recognition that stifles your empowerment training. Nevertheless, power or the beliefs you have about power are simply what you think about yourself.

Today, you have the opportunity to change the way you think about power or the lack of it. So train yourself to know that it is important to think that you are powerful rather than thinking of yourself as powerless.

TAKE THE TIME TO CHANGE YOUR LIFE

One of the most common misperceptions about changing your life is thinking that you don't have enough time. When you make the commitment to change the way you think, act, work, and live, you always have enough time. To take the first step to change your life, you must believe you can do it, which means that you have the time to do it. Time is a relative term used to place you in a niche of complacency and mediocrity. Your life is time-based because of your thoughts about it. Time has no power over you. It doesn't matter how old you are today or what type of condition you are in, you are still alive. And you will remain alive until your body ceases to function. During the time in between, you will spend your life-hours doing something. Why not spend them on empowering yourself to express greatness?

The vision of empowerment that you create for yourself must be free of time limitations. Your thoughts and actions must be present-moment ones. In other words, you must remove future thinking from your thoughts. When you can control your thoughts to live in the present moment, you free yourself of self-imposed limitations about your current abilities to change your life.

YOU HAVE THE TIME TO CHANGE YOUR LIFE.

It doesn't matter how long it takes to accomplish your goal. The important thing to remember is the joy of the journey itself.

Chapter Two
Self-Discovery

Your memories of the past prevent you from seeing today clearly.

The desire to change is a powerful force that you must reckon with if you want to change the way you think, act, work, and live. The undercurrent of power producing your desires connects you with a much higher power. If you search for this power, it will not only transform your life, it will lead you to your unconditioned, uncluttered, intuitive consciousness: a place where all things are possible. Unfortunately, far too many people believe this consciousness exists outside of them.

Nevertheless, the desire to change is the first step in the self-discovery process: a process you use to examine your life and develop an action plan to change it. The self-discovery process empowers you to go beyond the boundaries imposed on you by family, friends, and society. It leads you into another level of consciousness where you will face the challenges of establishing new, more complete relationships with other people.

What is the process for self-discovery? How does it happen? How do you go to this level of empowered awareness? The answer is quite simple: Start from where you are right now and move forward.

I. SELF-DISCOVERY

Many individuals who successfully change their lives begin with some type of self-discovery process. Self-discovery is nothing magical or difficult; it is the willingness of an individual to examine his or her life. If you are feeling impoverished, you seek wealth. If you are feeling ill, you seek good health. If you are unemployed, you seek a job. All of the challenges you feel today automatically seek a solution. The best solution to all your problems is found within your mind, your intuitive consciousness.

The moment you feel overpowered by illusions of poverty, unemployment, failure, addiction, and fear is the moment for you to discover why you feel this way. For many, the way to begin is by acknowledging that they have a problem. It's a problem to be treated with a sense of urgency, similar to the way you would treat a cancer spreading through your body. If it's left untreated, you can expect pernicious results.

When you become ill, you seek the services of a doctor to tell you what's ailing you and to prescribe a cure. The sickness of feeling stuck, helpless, and unable to change your life requires the services of a specialist: someone that's familiar with the problems in your life. Regardless of how many people you search for to solve your problems, you ultimately discover that you are the most qualified person to do it. So you must learn to heal yourself.

The time it takes to change your life is your time, not someone else's time. You cannot turn your challenges over to seminar leaders, spiritual deities, or political leaders, because they do not have the power to change your life. They can talk about resources that you can use to assist you with overcoming your problems. They tell you success stories, make promises, and extol you to believe everything will be all right. However, after awhile, you will realize that it is you who know exactly what's bothering you and what you need to do to solve the problems you are facing.

The information here is to simply motivate you to take action. Once you have the desire to act, there are some suggestions to assist you with creating a vision of empowerment. For most individuals, the greatest challenge in their lives is to change the behavior that causes them pain. For you to change, you must do something different from what you have been doing up to this point. Moreover, it really doesn't matter what it is as long as it's something different. Whenever you express something different from what you have been doing, it will produce a different outcome.

When you become uncomfortable with your life, you will seek

a way to change it. Most people seek ways to change their lives when they become uncomfortable with their present situation. The greater your discomfort, the stronger your desires to change. So ask yourself: Are you ready to change today, or will you wait until tomorrow? The answer depends on the present intensity of your desires. If you are truly unhappy with your present condition, then you are ready now to take the first step to change.

The moment you desire to change your life, your body shivers with fear. Just the thought of change sends burning waves of anxiety through your mind like a grass fire. The initial reaction of most people to change is to retreat to the comforts of complacency and apathy. Unfortunately, this bastion of failure and shattered dreams is no longer a refuge for you. You need something else to quench the burning desires of change scorching your mind.

Each day the morning sun brings with its light your vision to change. Within the sun's rays is the solution for all your problems. This day contains a bountiful supply of creative ideas sufficient to solve any problem you are facing. The question for you is: Do you treat these ideas with contempt, disdain, and familiarity because they come to you so freely?

Try, try, try, but you will quickly discover that an unhappy person cannot ignore his or her desires to change. They are too powerful for those besieged with lack, limitation, and struggle to ignore. Your desires exist to serve you and only you. They are the essence of your life. Without desires, you would cease to exist as a viable person. They represent your spiritual DNA. If you feel weak spiritually and materially, it is because you are manifesting weak and unfocused desires. If you feel strong and powerful, it is because you are manifesting strong and focused desires.

During moments of great despair in your life, you will find a plentiful supply of strong desires willing to step forward and lead you out of your despair. You must be willing to allow these desires into your life and treat them as your warriors. Like all great leaders, you need strong warriors to follow you into battle; however, they need you to guide them.

The choice to change is always yours to make.

On some days, the sun shines brightly on a gloomy mind that feels trapped in a hellhole of hopelessness. Each day provides you with the power to change your life by expressing the desires you have. Nevertheless, to overcome your present problems, you must choose your desires wisely, especially those desires that come to you unconditioned. You can use these unconditioned desires to perpetuate your continued despair or to create a totally different person.

Some of your desires appear to you according to the way you feel. If you feel tired, overcome with hopelessness, you will attract corresponding desires. These desires are undisciplined. They have no purpose except to keep you feeling the way you always feel, tired and helpless.

When you awaken with thoughts of grief and despair, it is time to focus on the desires that have the power to overcome the problems. Listen to the silent voices with the great power. The silent voices from your intuitive consciousness are your desires prodding you to do something with your life. Listen to them rather than the loud voices of spin doctors.

The power to change exists only within your mind. You truly are what you think. If you think you are weak and powerless, you act like it. If you think you are strong and powerful, you act thusly. Your thoughts express themselves within your desires. If you have no desires, it is because you have ignored your thoughts.

Today is the moment you make the decision to change your life. You want to do it now rather than putting it off for a later time. By acting now, you take the first step toward proclaiming your worthiness to express greatness.

Tomorrow is the playground for the weak and powerless. Today is the paradise where the great people live. So use today as your moment in time to express greatness. Don't daydream about what you will have tomorrow, when you can have it all now. Some people who have successfully diagnosed and treated their illness begin by writing all the symptoms (illusions) on a sheet of paper. They list all the obvious illusions in a random order without placing importance on any particular one. An example of this procedure may be described in this manner:

1. I have problems following through on my ideas.

2. I tend to discuss other people with disparaging comments.
3. I smoke too much weed.
4. I drink too much beer, wine, or whiskey.
5. I am very angry with people of different races.
6. I am afraid to admit that I am very ambitious.
7. I love to feel important around people.
8. I am shy around people.
9. I create a lot of debt without realizing that I am creating it.
10. I am selfish.

Naturally, you will include your own language and feelings to express those problems affecting your life. There are other methods you can also use to identify your problems.

Another method is to select the one challenge that seems to be causing you the greatest discomfort and focus your energies on this single challenge. In using the list above, let's suppose it is number one: *I have problems following through on my ideas.* After you think about this challenge for a moment, you clearly discern some of the obvious obstacles:

1. Procrastination.
2. Lack of commitment to the idea.
3. Fear of success and failure.
4. Unclear ideas.
5. Too many ideas.
6. Low self-esteem.
7. Self-imposed obstacles (lack of money, education, social

status, etc.).
8. Relying exclusively on prayer.
9. Seeking permission from others.
10. Seeking acceptance from others.

Now you are in a position to begin working on yourself. When you see your problems in written form, they appear to be somewhat overwhelming and daunting. That is one way to perceive your life; however, another way to perceive it is to understand that to change your life will take you a lifetime. As I said earlier, all the work you will do from this moment in time until your last breath as a human will require a devotion to the duty of self-empowerment. After all, you are going to do something with your time. So why not spend it in the manner you would like?

You can now begin with the first self-imposed obstacle on the above list:

1. PROCRASTINATION

What is procrastination? You might want to use the dictionary definition as a guide to begin the process. Some examples to consider are: "To postpone action." "To delay work on something you are required to do." You can also add: "To talk an idea to death." "To choke the life out of your ambition." Or, cynically: "To have ambition without drive."

To discover the true meaning requires a deeper understanding of exactly what's happening with you. There are specific things you do that interfere with your actions to express your ideas. There is something causing you to postpone or delay action on your ideas. The discovery of this cause will unleash all the power needed to move you forward to the next step.

Some individuals who have used this system discovered that the answers are found in the things you do to postpone or delay action. The causes are numerous: a few of them can be expressed this way:

1. I seek approval from others (family, friends, spouse, coworkers, etc.) to validate my ideas.
2. I lose confidence in my idea very easily, especially when someone does not support it favorably or enthusiastically.
3. I develop other ideas that seem more important.
4. I become distracted with outside activities (television, sports, entertainment, male-female relationships, and family issues).
5. I spend too much time drinking alcohol, overeating, and smoking weed.

The solution to overcoming procrastination is to understand that it is nothing more than a way of life to which you have become accustomed. Procrastination takes the same amount of thought as courage and action. You have to condition your mind to act even though you might be concerned about the results. The cure for procrastination is action—the action you take to complete an idea and not the action you take to kill the idea.

You can further examine the five areas you identified above

and gain insights into their true impact on your behavior.

(1). APPROVAL

You could say it's normal for someone to seek support or approval for his or her ideas. As a child, you raise your hand in the classroom, anxious for the teacher to call on you for the answer. There is a certain joy in having the right answer. It motivates you. It builds your confidence, and it inspires you to raise your hand again and again as long as you continue to receive the teacher's approval.

When you raise your hand and the teacher calls on you for the answer and you give the incorrect one, it causes embarrassment. You feel your esteem plunge to new lows that weaken your confidence in yourself. After continuous incorrect answers, you begin to question, to doubt yourself. This doubtful environment becomes a fertile field for intellectual stagnation, which kills your creativity.

(2). CONFIDENCE

A child learns to walk because of confidence. He has the confidence that he can walk like all the other people around him. And regardless of what people say, the child will keep falling and getting up until he succeeds in walking. That is the essence of confidence. You must continue to work toward your goals no matter how many times you fail. You must raise your hand and express your thoughts no matter how many times you give incorrect answers.

Self-Discovery

The confidence you have in your abilities affects all your decisions. The decision to change your life cannot occur without confidence in your ability to change your life. The more work you do on your goal, the greater your confidence grows. The secret to everything in the universe is contained in confidence. Nothing happens without it. Creativity is not possible without confidence.

(3). UNFOCUSED

As the saying goes, "Too many cooks spoil the soup." Well, the same is true for ideas. Too many ideas at the same time will overwhelm you and plunge you into inactivity. Several ideas at the same time represent an out-of-control mind. An unfocused mind wanders from place to place without stopping long enough to work on the goal at hand.

The obvious solution to an unfocused mind is a focused one. Needless to say, this is easier said than done. A cluttered, unfocused mind is a haven for daydreamers. It brings them great pleasure to discuss all the things they want to do someday, or all the things they could have done if. . . .

The key thing to remember is to control your actions so you express what you really want and not a substitute. The most dangerous thing in your life is an unfocused desire. An unfocused desire can create havoc in your life because it is allowed to exist without a guide or teacher. You must accept yourself as the person who knows exactly what you want to achieve in your life. This makes you the guide that illumines your thoughts to express desires that are consistent with your vision to achieve success and empowerment.

The person with unfocused desires is a victim of circumstances. He or she lives in the darkness of fear, poverty, struggle, and doubt. All of these emotions cause pain and discomfort. They are the enemies of change. For you to change your life, you must conquer these emotions and make them your slaves. Yes, slaves, who will obey your commands.

The joy of change is found in a focused, goal-oriented mind. Whoever possesses such a treasure will achieve success. Nothing can stand in the way of a focused mind.

(4). OUTSIDE ACTIVITIES

After a hard day's work, you want to do something to relax. Perhaps go to a movie, watch television, have a drink, smoke some weed, listen to music, or head to the gym for a workout. Most individuals find one or more of these types of activities to assuage their tired bodies. Over and over again, they repeat themselves in your life. And over and over again, you continue to need them for relaxation.

A tired body—mentally and physically—suffers greatly when it cannot find some way to rejuvenate itself. The mind accepts outside activities similar to the way a body accepts food: it craves them. And as with the body, too much of something will make you ill.

Some people believe that a good way to unwind and recharge your batteries is to have a drink with the fellows or girls. So you push, push yourself during the day to reward yourself in the evening with a drink or two with your friends. It obviously doesn't take very long for you to realize that this activity will adversely affect you.

There are no outside activities. Everything you do, every comment you make, every smile or frown you give, is an expression of your inner thoughts. YOU ARE YOUR ACTIONS. So the thought of something happening outside of you without your approval is an illusion.

All your activities become your addictions. In this case, you and your activities are one, but your activities are greater than you. You have to change this to the following: You and your activities are one, but you are greater than your activities.

(5). ADDICTIONS

What's the harm in having a couple of drinks after a hard day's work? Why not have a few hits of marijuana, some methamphetamine, or some cocaine? What about having a couple of cheeseburgers and fries and ice cream to satisfy your hunger? This makes you feel good.

Those individuals who are victimized by their addictions and who take the first step to overcome them realize that they are victimized by their thoughts and actions. They also know that greatness is achieved by changing the way they think of themselves.

The true adherents to this principle always succeed, because they know they are worthy to express greatness. For you to join with them, you must visualize your success from a victim-free consciousness.

As you can clearly discern from your evaluation of procrastination, it is a very difficult problem to overcome. You need a strong commitment to your inner power to stop procrastinating.

2. LACK OF COMMITMENT TO THE IDEA

What happens to your great ideas? If you stop for a moment and reflect on the numerous great ideas you have had in your life so far, you would probably wonder what happened to them.

Whenever you have a great idea, you feel a certain excitement throughout your body. You believe you have something wonderful to share with the world or something to make you wealthy or get you a job promotion. The initial response you have to a great idea is overwhelming gratitude for the opportunity to accomplish something wonderful.

In the meanwhile, you begin to delve into the *how to* express this idea, and that's when you realize there are some difficulties involved in expressing it. The *how to* do it usually stops many people from moving forward with their ideas. In many instances, you are able to clearly discern that you have a fragile idea. When you have a fragile idea, it means you lack a strong commitment to it.

Self-Discovery

For you to express your ideas in the visible world, you must have a strong, unshakable commitment to them. When you have anything less than a strong commitment to your ideas, you will only produce deeper feelings of failure and helplessness.

3. FEAR OF SUCCESS AND FAILURE

Today, you can perceive yourself as being either a success or a failure. You have the power to create countless images of yourself. The power of your mind determines how you interpret the decisions you make and what you think about your present conditions.

When you find yourself in an unpleasant position in your life, you probably feel like you have failed. When your decisions produce unwelcome setbacks, you feel the sting of failure overwhelm your desires for success. For you to achieve success in your life, you first must clearly know you are already successful. The success you seek is not something outside of yourself, but the thought processes you use to create different images of yourself. The important thing to remember about success and failure is that you are always successful and never a failure. Regardless of the number of times you are rejected, fired, divorced, or unable to obtain money, fame, and recognition from others, you must acknowledge and confirm that you are successful. It is what you think about yourself that determines your actions.

4. UNCLEAR IDEAS

When you are feeling down and out and unable to come up

with a great idea, you must refrain from accepting any idea that comes to you. Frequently, ideas born of minds besieged with worry and anxiety are unclear ones. To change the way you feel about yourself, you must clear your mind of the images that reveal you as a helpless and powerless person.

A clear idea is a vision of empowerment. You have no doubts about its authenticity. An unclear idea is weak, fuzzy, and difficult to grasp. It gives you an iffy feeling, a feeling that it might not work. With this type of idea, you should hit the brakes and stop. For you to pursue an unclear idea is for you to welcome more problems into your life.

So remember to avoid acting on unclear ideas at all costs. It is better not to take any action until you are able to clear your mind so you can clearly form a vision of your goal and how to implement it.

5. TOO MANY IDEAS

When your confidence and self-esteem are low, you might feel the need to develop several ideas at one time. Too many ideas, like too many cooks, will undoubtedly spoil your vision. Whenever you have too many ideas, more than one at a time, you undoubtedly don't have great confidence in the success of your ideas.

Let's imagine that you desire to start a new business. A friend invites you over to his or her house to discuss an investment opportunity. When you arrive at your friend's house, there are ten people already there. Your friend welcomes you to the meeting by telling you it's an investment club.

Everyone there touts the possibilities of making a great return on your investment. You become interested and decide to invest some of the money you have saved to start your business.

A couple of weeks later, while you're setting up your business, a coworker tells you about a neighborhood meeting to discuss the merits of a fast-food restaurant setting up close to the neighborhood. You agree to attend the meeting. After considerable discussion by all the people present, they agree to formalize the group by electing officers. Your coworker nominates you to become the leader of the association. You are unanimously elected.

Now it's time for you to develop your new business, a consultant business that provides business agents to represent professional athletes. You quickly discover you don't have the time and energy to participate in an investment club and neighborhood association and also start your business.

Nevertheless, out of deference to the people involved, you continue to participate in the two groups. You can't find the strength to say no, even though the two new ventures distract you from establishing your business, which is your original goal. So you delay the start of your business, hoping things will improve so that you can start it later. Unfortunately, too many ideas at the same time will stop you from working on your primary goal.

6. LOW SELF-ESTEEM

The death of all action is low self-esteem. Whenever you devalue yourself, you lose confidence in your abilities to achieve success. For many people, it is very difficult to recognize they have low self-esteem. Some people act confidently in certain areas and insecure and unsure of themselves in other areas. For example, a great athlete displays a high level of self-esteem and confidence in his or her profession. That same athlete, when placed in a high-level corporate boardroom or prestigious university, might find it difficult to express the same level of confidence and high self-esteem in the different environment.

There are degrees of low self-esteem. For you to succeed in changing the way you think and live requires you to have high self-esteem in all your actions. This requires you to become one with your new vision of yourself with power. It is your ability to accept yourself with power that will provide you with high self-esteem. Similarly, it is your unwillingness to accept yourself with power that creates low self-esteem.

For most individuals, money increases their self-esteem and the absence of it decreases their self-esteem. When you believe that external things such as money, fame, and material possessions give you power, you weaken your resolve to change the way you think and live. The solution to low self-esteem is power: the power that is found in your mind.

7. SELF-IMPOSED OBSTACLES

When you discover you are responsible for the problems in your life, you also know that to overcome those problems you must remove the obstacles that keep you tied to them. You discover the obstacles in your life by examining the cause of your problems. This examination will clearly reveal to you that your obstacles are illusions and you are the source of their existence.

As the creator of everything in your life, including the obstacles expressing themselves in your life as lack, limitation, fear, doubt, and struggle, you are also responsible for removing them from your life.

The obstacles in your life today are easily overcome whenever you decide to change the way you presently think and live. If you don't have an adequate amount of money to acquire the material things you desire, you can do something about it by believing you can do something about it. You can develop a plan, a strategy, and a commitment to achieving success.

The thought of achieving success is a daunting one for someone who believes he or she is powerless. When you confirm your poverty, you confirm the lack in your life. When you confirm your obstacles, you confirm the limitations in your life. When you confirm the fears in your life, you confirm the doubts in your life. When you confirm the struggle in your life, you confirm the powerlessness in your life. These beliefs become the bases for your self-imposed obstacles, while your new actions become the bases for you to achieve a new way to think and live.

8. RELYING EXCLUSIVELY ON PRAYER

When you feel powerless because of your problems, you naturally seek a way to overcome them. Many consciously poor individuals turn to religion and prayer to help them overcome their problems. Unfortunately, many individuals who have relied on religion and prayer to solve their problems have created a social, political, and economic dependency on them. This practice causes them to rely on religion and prayer rather than on themselves to solve everyday problems that victimize their lives.

To overcome a seemingly insoluble problem, you need to know that it is you who must take the action to solve the problem. The tools of religion and prayer are available to assist you with taking the necessary actions to overcome the problems in your life. Tools are instruments for you to use; however, they are useless unless you use them. For example, you can use some tools to build houses, airplanes, automobiles, and countless other things. If you use the proper tools, then the work is less cumbersome.

Religion and prayer are tools available for you to use to motivate and encourage yourself to have confidence in your abilities to solve the problems in your life. You must clearly know that your tools cannot do anything without you doing the work.

There isn't anything right or wrong about prayer and religion, except for those who believe they can use them to magically overcome depression, failure, and emotional pain. For the enlightened mind, both prayer and religion are very worthwhile tools to use to change your life, if they are properly used with other actions. You cannot use them alone to solve the problems you have created in your life. You must use the great power within your mind to do that.

9. SEEKING PERMISSION FROM OTHERS

On your journey to discover the power you have to change the way you think, act, work, and live, you will have moments when you distrust yourself. During those moments when you feel isolated and unsure of yourself, there will be a tendency to seek guidance from others on whether you should continue on your journey.

There are usually some people in your life that you respect and admire for their accomplishments. You value these individuals' opinions about you. You seek their advice on matters of great importance to you. If they say it is okay to move forward with an idea, it gives you comfort and confidence. Conversely, if they say you shouldn't move forward with your idea, it might cause you to second-guess yourself. These individuals represent your support system.

There is another support system available to you. This one is far greater than your current one, because it advises you on how to change your life. This is a support system of one, you. You can use it whenever you want because it is within your mind—intuitive consciousness—where you will find this great support system that will give you the necessary power to change the way you think and live.

You must know that you do not need permission from anyone, except you, to change the way you think and live. Someone told me a few months ago, "It is better to beg forgiveness than to ask for permission." It is better for you to take action based on your ideas rather than asking someone else's permission.

10. SEEKING ACCEPTANCE FROM OTHERS

When you seek permission from someone, you are also seeking acceptance from him or her. You are asking someone to accept what you are doing to change your life. You will discover that family and friends accept you according to the way you act. If you have established a victim relationship with them, it will be difficult for them to initially accept your new behavior. You will have to embody your new beliefs and express them in the way you think and live before someone will be able to take you seriously. Then, and only then, will others accept you as someone who thinks for himself or herself.

It is common practice among people who have lived powerless lifestyles to seek approval from others. If you are working on a project, you want your supervisor or colleagues to compliment you for your work. In those instances when you don't receive their compliments, you probably feel like they don't appreciate your hard work.

On this journey, you must move beyond the need for others

to accept you and your work. You must become your own approval agent. The judgments about success and failure are merely interpretations you use to measure your actions and the actions of others. When you remove the thoughts you have about success and failure, you automatically overcome the need to seek acceptance from others.

Seeds from the Ashes

Chapter Three
The Higher Self

You have to go beyond the problem to find the solution.

One of the greatest challenges you face each day is how to express the power within you. The years of struggling to survive the oppressive illusions in your life may have caused you to doubt your ability to overcome your present feelings of powerlessness. Yet today, in the midst of overwhelming perceptions of yourself with less power than you really possess, you have the opportunity to solve all your problems.

The process to unleash this great power is one that requires you to look inward and discover the source for solving all your problems. For you to become a part of this empowerment process, you must first learn to be comfortable with yourself and to overcome the belief that authentic power exists outside of your mind. You must condition your mind to know that all power comes from your mind.

Whenever you hear someone say something about inner power, do you really understand what it means or what it feels like beyond the sound of the words? The search for inner power is a continuous process that involves you working to overcome the problems in your life. This involvement requires you to go beyond the meaningless words and learn how to embody the greatness within you.

One way to begin this process is to free your mind to communicate with your higher consciousness. This method of communicating will allow you to ascribe voices and attributes to your thoughts. You can illustrate this practice by creating a dialogue between your lower self (victim consciousness) and your higher self (empowered consciousness, or your Sage).

For some people it is difficult to communicate with themselves. It is much easier to imagine that you are talking to another individual. You can do whatever makes you feel comfortable as long as you realize that the conversation is occurring in your mind. The purpose here is to guide you into trusting your intuitive power and for you to know that all power comes from within you. Even when you pray or meditate to a higher power, it is you that is doing the communicating and it is also you interpreting the answers to your prayers.

The point of changing how you think and live is to know you are responsible for doing the work. This self-responsibility changes the traditional relationship between the victim and the Creator, where the victim asks the Creator to solve a problem for him or her and believes that the Creator will accept the responsibility and do the work for him or her.

The task before you is for you to solve your own problems, because you are the one who created them. I'm sure you believe the illusions are responsible for the way you think and live. Unfortunately, in many ways, you are correct in the sense that you have given great power to other people and given yourself very little, if any, power.

Ask yourself: Who is responsible for someone who is a drug addict or alcoholic? Who is responsible for someone who is illiterate, unemployed, or homeless? Who is responsible for someone who is a murderer, thief, robber, or child molester? Who is responsible for the oppression and cruelty that someone experiences every day? The simple answer is the person who is taking and receiving the actions.

Anyone who allows himself or herself to think that someone else has control of their thoughts is a prime candidate to become a successful victim. Your mind is the gateway to your freedom. If you allow people to fill it with thoughts about how weak and powerless you are and how strong and powerful they are, you will remain helpless.

When you imagine yourself with power, you have power. The method to imagine yourself with power is to know you are able to talk directly to the power that can solve all your problems. Whenever you talk, pray, or meditate to a higher consciousness, you believe you are communicating with someone who has the power to give you something you desire, but have been unable to achieve.

The exercise you are about to do is a reflection of how it feels to see your thoughts on paper. During this process, you are praying or meditating to a higher consciousness with the power to solve your problems or fulfill your desires.

For you to change the way you think and live, you must open your mind to travel deep into the bowels of human knowledge and beyond. The more you work on overcoming your problems, the more comfortable you will become with trusting the power in your mind. This discovery of consciousness will lead you into pure enlightenment; however, to achieve this great power, you must first learn to talk to your higher consciousness.

You can begin the process by relaxing your thoughts, banishing your fears, and knowing that you have the power to change the way you think and live. This belief alone is sufficient to stimulate you to action.

A CONVERSATION WITH YOUR HIGHER SELF

"Who is it?" I ask, startled for a moment.

"It is I," says the voice from within the lights. "I am the one you seek."

"Are you the Creator?"

"I am that I am. That is who I am."

"Oh, my God, it's the Creator," I exclaim. "But—I thought I would see Sage first?"

"Don't you recognize me?" the voice says calmly.

"Uh, I'm not sure. Who are you?"

"It is I, Sage, your friend."

"Sage—but I thought you said you were the Creator."

"I am the Creator. When you see me in this form you also see the Creator."

"Really!"

"Yes, the Creator and I are one at this level of consciousness. Here, I am empowered to conceive myself as both Creator and human."

"Do you mean I have been with the Creator for this long and didn't know it?"

"Yes, Advocate, that's true," Sage says, calmly embracing me with his thoughts. "As you know, you have the power to conceive yourself as both God and man."

"Yeah, I do."

"That's good."

"But Sage—How does it work?"

"It works when you achieve clear awareness," he says. "When

your thoughts are clear, your awareness of yourself as a human diminishes."

"In what way?"

"It is your awareness of yourself with so many limitations that prevents you from becoming aware of yourself as the Creator"

"But—I don't understand."

"When you free your mind of self-imposed limitations, you empower yourself to think as a creator."

"How do I overcome my limitations?"

"By changing the way you think about yourself and the things you desire to achieve."

"I have tried to do this, but somehow I seem to always discover new limitations."

"Trust the creative process and know that you have the power within you," Sage says. "Don't look for this power outside of you."

"But I don't know how to control my runaway thoughts yet"

"I know."

"Then?"

"When you recognize my presence in your thoughts, you will see your life clearly," Sage says. "I am your unconditioned consciousness. I have the power to condition my thoughts to become many different life forms."

"Uh, that is true, but I don't feel this power in me right now," I say silently. "Right now, I am aware of being a human being.

Nothing else overshadows this awareness."

"That's because you think with your conditioned consciousness," Sage replies. "As a human, you think of yourself with limitations—"

"Well, I do—I mean, I guess I do have limitations."

"Only self-imposed ones."

"Well, that's true," I say. "But I can't seem to think beyond my limitations."

"That's why you are here now so that you can learn to think of yourself without limitations," Sage says, comforting my thoughts.

"At this level of consciousness, you will begin to think of yourself as a creator rather than as a human creation."

"But I am human."

"Okay, let's go beyond the human awareness for a moment," Sage says, moving his thoughts to a higher level of human awareness. "We are going to discover the secrets of power that will allow you to never be powerless again regardless of the magnitude of your problems."

"I am ready," I exclaim excitedly.

"Good! I am sure you will agree that it was your ignorance about who you thought you were that prevented you from recognizing the Creator and me as part of your thoughts."

"That's right, "

"Now," Sage assures me, "you will learn to recognize our presence in your thoughts. This will give you great power, because we will share our power with you."

"Does this mean I will discover my purpose?"

"No," Sage says. "It means you are ready to receive more information about your purpose."

"Uh, I'm sure you know that I'm ready," I say, while I focus on controlling my thoughts.

"Very good!" Sage says, complimenting my grasp of his thoughts. "However, before you receive such powerful information, information that will give you dominion over your life, you must first master the knowledge of how to overcome the illusions—"

"Excuse me, Sage: Is that it?"

"Yes, that's it," Sage says. "When you accomplish this task, I will return to your thoughts with great power and clarity. Then you will have all the power you need to fulfill your purpose—"

"How long will this take?" I ask.

"Not long. You're almost there."

"That's what I wanted to hear."

The conversation with yourself is simply your mind communicating with your higher self, your intuitive consciousness. This process of conversing with yourself is a way for you to see what you are thinking. Imagine for a moment that you wrote on paper your prayers and meditations. How do you think they would look and sound?

The further you go in developing your mind to think beyond your limitations, the closer you get to expressing your greatness.

REVIEW OF HIGHER CONSCIOUSNESS EXERCISE

1. How do you feel when you pray or meditate?
2. Do you believe or feel that you're talking to a higher being inside or outside of you?
3. What do you usually expect to accomplish by prayer or meditation?
4. The Sage in the exercise is you expressing empowerment.
5. The Creator is the unconditioned consciousness with the power to express limitless ideas and expressions of life.
6. The unenlightened requestor is you expressing doubts about your power to change your life.
7. The process of change flows from the individual entering into a prayer-meditative state of mind to the prayer itself and finally to the realization that you have the power to solve all your problems.
8. The results of prayer-meditation are expressed in the confidence you have in yourself, not in the belief that a higher power is not present within you.

Seeds from the Ashes

Chapter Four
Love

I know how to love the saint and the murderer as I love myself.

When you search within yourself for the solutions to a problem, you inevitably discover that one of the greatest challenges you face is your inability to express unconditional love. The key to solving all problems is your ability to express unconditional love in all your actions. For you to solve even simple problems, you first need to know how to love others unconditionally, without any judgments.

For many victims of life, love is simply a word defined in a dictionary. It is a soft whisper from your mother's lips as she cuddles you. It is something you use to seduce, disarm, and manipulate other people. It is both endearing and destructive. Love is whatever you believe it is.

Love is the source of your power to think, to express ideas, to watch birds fly, to smell flowers, to taste honey, to feel the soft touch of a woman's body, and to listen to smooth music in a blissful silence. Love is everywhere and in everybody.

For you, the seeker of the power to change your life, the search for love is a never-ending journey. It is an unfolding drama of success and failure. It's a search that will take you into the darkness of your consciousness, a place where no one goes except you. Yet it is from the darkness and solitude of your mind that you will find unconditional love and the power to change your life.

The inner search for power requires a clear and focused mind. To begin this process, you must be willing to sever your ties to your former behavior. This step will allow you to remain steadfast in your search and avoid the pitfalls of becoming sidetracked by what you see and hear from others in your life. You must be willing to go beyond the conditional love that victims use to live their lives.

To understand the value of unconditional love, you first must understand the folly of embodying conditional love. The former is permanent, unchangeable, while the latter is transitory, changeable, and whimsical. When you examine each one with a careful intuitive eye, you are able to see how they affect your behavior.

CONDITIONAL LOVE

A good example of conditional love is marriage. During the

marriage ceremony, both parties express a deep love and commitment to each other "until death do us part." For many marriages, after the ceremony and living together for several years, the blissful union turns into a hate-filled nightmare of intense pain and suffering, which ultimately leads to separation and divorce. Someone might ask the participants: What happened to your love? Why did it turn to hate? They might look at you bewildered, searching their mind for answers to something they know little, if anything, about.

Conditional love is evasive because it is so much a part of the emotional fabric that shapes our behavior with other people. Conditional love is a victim's love, the type of love that interferes with the way you solve problems. The longer you work on searching for the answers within you, the more clearly you will understand that a victim's love is conditional, fragile, and fleeting.

The core of conditional love is a moral selfishness that controls how you think about yourself and others. This moral selfishness teaches you how to love others conditionally by giving and removing your love according to the way you feel at any given time. Victims relish this power because they believe it is all the power they can possess.

In the example of marriage, you can remove your love just by thinking about it. Zap! It is gone just like that. Where did it go? If you look closely within the victim's mind, you will discover that it didn't go anywhere: It was merely redirected to someone else.

When you remove your love from a single individual, you remove it from all individuals. By doing this, you in essence affirm your commitment to conditional love. This commitment to conditional love imprisons you in victim consciousness with beliefs of fear, isolation, and distrust of strangers.

When you condition your mind to live in the darkness of emotional isolation, fear, and distrust for too long, you lose the power to love yourself and others. This lost love becomes a fertile haven for anger, hatred, and intense emotional and psychological pain. The absence of love destroys the ability to feel, to care, and to love yourself and others unconditionally. These emotionally void feelings create a façade to hide the fears and distrust you have toward others.

The truth about what lurks behind the victim's façade of love is a lovesick, frightened person who searches for conditional lovers to satisfy his or her quest for love. This addictive search leads someone to prowl the streets, sit innocently looking in church pews, and wait patiently on bar stools for his or her next victim. Once a suitable prey is found, he or she is showered with endearing platitudes of love encapsulated with feelings of grandeur. For the victim, this is love.

UNCONDITIONAL LOVE

As you work on changing your life and solving your everyday problems, searching for unconditional love might seem silly or irrelevant. Yet the secret to changing your life is to understand

how you feel about yourself and other people. For example, you might ask yourself:
- Do I really love my wife or husband?
- Do I love her or him unconditionally?
- Do I know how unconditional love feels?
- Have I ever felt it?
- Do I love my children? My friends?

The search for love is a pilgrimage down many different emotional roads. Some of the roads are covered with deleterious illusions hidden behind the actions of individuals with malevolent intentions. On every street, you notice them lurking nearby in emotional darkness, waiting for the right moment for you to invite them into your life.

The reasons for you to distrust everyone you meet are omnipresent in your thoughts, because the cornerstone of the victim consciousness you are working to overcome is distrust, particularly distrust of strangers.

Meanwhile, as you continue on your journey to find unconditional love, you must be strong enough to overcome the persistent questions about whom you can trust. Some of the questions you might ask yourself:
- Why can't I find love?
- How did other enlightened individuals find love?
- How did they get through this maze of loneliness and conflicting beliefs?

- What is the key that opens the mind to embrace unconditional love?
- Why do I erect an emotional barrier between strangers and me?

During your journey of self-discovery, you will undoubtedly have many questions regarding your progress to express unconditional love. If you are not strongly committed to changing your life, these types of questions may cause you to abandon your search. If this happens to you, you must not panic. You must stop and reaffirm your commitment to your goal of creating a new way to think and live. You must also become secure enough with your inner power to trust strangers to come into your life.

Whenever you feel alienated from family and friends because of your search to empower yourself, you must focus on your desires, not the judgments of others. You must know, or believe until you reach the point of knowing, that unconditional love is present in everyone you see, including strangers. For you to see it in yourself and others, you must overcome the victim beliefs you have about other people.

The ability to trust strangers is a liberating feeling of having *real* power. Nevertheless, while you continue working to change your perceptions of strangers, they continue to pass through your mind like birds of prey. You see them on the subway, in restaurants, at the theater, walking on sidewalks, and passing by in speeding cars. You only glance at most of them. Some of them stop to talk and introduce themselves as loving, caring people. Naturally, you are skeptical of their motives because you don't know them.

When you carefully examine your victim beliefs, it seems odd for a stranger to love another stranger without some type of hidden agenda. How do you love someone you don't have a long-term relationship with? This seems like it's impossible. Yet it might seem equally impossible to many victims for you to find and express unconditional love.

For most victims, the ability of someone to express unconditional love is unbelievable. Although many victims think so, the search for unconditional love is not a difficult one. All it takes to get you started is a desire. From this single desire, you will learn how to empower your mind to go beyond victim consciousness and enter into the process of achieving unconditional love. The following anecdote is an example of this process.

ANECDOTE FOR ACHIEVING LOVE

The purpose of this anecdote is to train your mind to see limitless possibilities, to learn how to embody the principles of love, and to empower your thoughts to go beyond your current level of awareness. This mind transformation process will guide you deeper into your higher consciousness. This higher consciousness is the Clear Access Process (CAP) consciousness. CAP consciousness is that part of your mind where your thoughts are clear and free of illusions.

In CAP consciousness you are able to see life more clearly. This clarity will allow you to examine this anecdote and compare it to your own experiences with trying to love someone who has caused you great pain and suffering.

As you relax your thoughts, imagine yourself traveling through time to the year 1876, in a place called Arizona. It is here that you will observe Burning Tree, a Native American, who is training to become a warrior in his tribe.

Burning Tree is a unique man. He lives in harmony with the things around him. He loves deer, snakes, birds, horses, people, and all life as a part of himself. He feels their pain, joy, sorrow, and purpose. He believes he is one with them.

Today, Burning Tree has completed his training to become a warrior, albeit a reluctant one, because he cannot bring himself to kill another human or any life form. Fortunately, no one knows how strongly he feels about preserving all life forms. So, while he and the eleven other warrior-initiates bask in the joy of their impending coronation as warriors, he suddenly hears screams. He turns startled toward the screams and sees several women and children running screaming toward him. At first, he doesn't recognize the young girl as his sister, Yellow Flower.

"Help! Help! Please help me!" Yellow Flower shouts, struggling to maintain her balance.

"What happened?" Burning Tree shouts, reaching for her hand.

"They killed mamma," she sobs.

"What—What do you say—"

"Yes, my brother, she is dead."

"No, no, no, I don't believe it," the warriors shout. "Where is she? Show us!"

"Give me a moment to gather my thoughts," Yellow Flower says, shaking her head in disbelief.

"Forgive us, my sister," the warriors comfort her. "We just want to know who killed her."

"I don't know," Yellow Flower sobs. "They were palefaces."

Yellow Flower, Burning Tree, and the others stand helpless, talking among themselves and sobbing. After several minutes, Chief Straight Arrow arrives and Yellow Flower tells him what happened. He places his arm around her and says, "Burning Tree, I want you and the other new warriors to go get your mother's body and bring it back to the village. Then you must find the palefaces and bring them to me."

Burning Tree and the other warriors race to get his mother's body. They quickly find her mangled, lifeless body about a half a mile from their village. Burning Tree stares in horror at his mother's naked body, her face beaten beyond recognition. He kneels to cover her body. "Mamma, mamma," he shouts, kneeling to lift her body. "Mamma, say something—"

"C'mon, Burning Tree," one of the warriors shouts angrily, placing his arm around Burning Tree's shoulder. "We have to take her body back to the chief."

They lift her body gently onto the buffalo-skin blanket and carry her back slowly to the village. On the way back, Burning Tree begins to experience a strange sensation. He feels an emptiness in his body that's greater than his mother's death. This painful feeling grows in intensity with each step he takes. Little by little he feels a piece of his soul slip away.

Several minutes later, they arrive at the village with his mother's body. The entire village rushes to them, seeking answers about what happened to their fallen sister, Grey Dove. As they get closer, they suddenly see the horror contained within her lifeless body, a horror so great that a great cry of anguish erupts from among the village people.

"Why? Why? Why?" the women wail over and over. "Who did this horrible deed to our beloved sister?"

"We don't know," the men cry loudly. "Let's find the murderers and kill them."

"Kill them! Kill them! Kill them!" the entire village shouts over and over.

A stunned Burning Tree hears their shouts and suddenly remembers what is causing the emptiness in his mind: it is the absence of anger. He isn't angry with the palefaces for killing his mother, because he realizes that his mother is not dead, but alive and well in another consciousness.

After several minutes of total silence, Burning Tree extends his hands toward the sky and says, "We cannot allow hate and anger to consume our hearts. We must pursue these men with love in our hearts so that when we find them we will act from a position of love rather than anger and hate."

"You must be crazy," Strong Bear shouts. "The only love we are going to show them will come from our tomahawks, because when we find them we're going to scalp them."

"Scalp them! Scalp them!" the warriors shout in unison.

"No, no, no, I beg you—"

"I'm sorry, Burning Tree, but I'm afraid I have to agree with the warriors," Chief Straight Arrow says, nodding his head in agreement. "Now, go and find the killers and bring honor to our fallen sister, Grey Dove, and to our village."

Burning Tree reluctantly joins the other warriors as they arm themselves to search for the killers. Afterward, they spread out and meticulously search for nearly four hours before they see the two men sitting beside a campfire several miles from their village. The warriors scatter and encircle the men. When they are within fifty yards, they suddenly attack, screaming, "Kill them! Kill them!"

The warriors pounce on the surprised men. The men kneel and begin pleading for their lives. "Please don't kill us," pleads the man with the missing front teeth and long, dirty blond hair. "Take what you want, but don't kill us."

"Silence, palefaces," Running Bear says, placing his spear on the man's throat. "Shut up, and stay down on your knees, palefaces."

The men continue pleading for their lives. The warriors become irritated, and several of them shout, "Let's kill them now."

"No," Running Bear shouts, "We're going to take them back to the chief. He will decide what we should do with them."

The warriors finally relent and agree with Running Bear. They bind the men with leather straps and drag them back to the village. Burning Tree joins them; however, he remains silent during the trip back to the village.

When they arrive at the village, everyone gathers quickly around the men shouting, "Kill them!"

The warriors quickly form a protective shield around the men. Running Bear asks a young boy standing nearby to go and get the chief. The boy races like a horse to get the chief. When he arrives at the chief's teepee, the boy shouts, "Chief, come quickly. They have found the men who killed Grey Dove."

"Good," the chief says. "Let's go and see what they have to say before we kill them."

"We didn't do anything," the younger one pleads. "Why are you doing this to us?"

The chief and the boy walk silently, with the chief walking several feet in front of the boy. The chief stops suddenly and says, "Go get Yellow Flower. Tell her to meet me at the Council of Chiefs' table."

When Chief Straight Arrow reaches the Council of Chiefs' table, the high-ranking elders seated at the table stand and honor his presence. The chief acknowledges their presence and takes his seat as the head of the council. He then orders the men brought before the council.

Several of the older warriors bring the bound, sobbing, and frightened palefaces before the council and order them to kneel and remain silent.

"Silence!" the chief shouts. "Bring Yellow Flower here. And Burning Tree, you come and stand next to me."

As Yellow Flower and Burning Tree walk toward the chief, the men appear startled at the sight of Yellow Flower. The chief takes Yellow Flower's hand and calmly says, "Are these the men that raped and killed Grey Dove?"

"Yes," she sobs, "they did it. I saw them kill my mother."

"Please," the men plead in unison, "we don't know what she's talking about."

"Silence!" the chief admonishes the men. "You don't speak until I tell you. Anyway, I believe Yellow Flower." The chief and the elders whisper among themselves for a few minutes, and the chief says, "We have decided to place the palefaces' lives in the hands of Burning Tree."

Meanwhile, a stunned and shocked Burning Tree looks at the chief with disbelief. He is frozen in the moment, unable to speak. He had expected the chief to make the decision. As he scans the faces of the members of the tribe, he hears the chants of "Kill them" echoing in his thoughts. They want him to kill the men and avenge his mother's death.

Burning Tree continues to search for answers in the faces of his brethren, but all he sees is their anger and hatred for the palefaces. He decides to close his eyes and seek the answers from within his thoughts. He goes peacefully within his thoughts to a place where he feels the presence of universal love. He knows that love for all life is greater than the pleasures of vengeance and murder. He opens his eyes and says, "Let them go. I forgive them."

"No, no," the crowd roars angrily. "We don't care what Burning Tree says, we are going to kill them."

The chief rises and says, "No, it is his decision, and we must honor it. Release them!" The warriors release the men, and the chief says, "Go palefaces, go. Don't ever return here again or we will kill you."

The men run quickly from the village. They run as fast as they can to their campsite. Afterward, they laugh and ridicule the actions of Burning Tree. "Ain't that Injun crazy?" the younger one says.

"Yeah," the gap-toothed one laughs. "Let's get the hell out of here before they change their minds."

"Naw, we can spend the night here and leave bright and early in the morning."

"Okay. Let's get some shut-eye."

Meanwhile, Burning Tree takes his sister's hand, and they walk over to his mother's body. As he walks slowly past the villagers, he feels their pain and anguish. It is pain and anguish created from generations of suffering and oppression. He looks into his mother's lifeless face and sees himself frozen in their memories. This is the moment he realizes that his friends and supporters have lived with anger and hatred for so long that they no longer know how to love their enemies.

Later that night, shortly before going to sleep, the men who killed Burning Tree's mother celebrate their freedom by drinking, eating, and laughing at how they had made a fool out of Burning Tree. While they bask in their celebration, three renegade warriors suddenly attack and kill the two men.

Early the next morning as the sun is rising, Burning Tree awakens and walks to the entrance of his teepee. He looks first to the dawning of life, and then he looks to the ground and sees two human scalps. He immediately knows that the scalps belong to the two palefaces who killed his mother.

He bends down and picks up the two scalps. He feels the moisture of blood and raises the scalps toward the blue sky and cries loudly to the spirits, "Forgive them, for they don't understand how to express forgiveness."

Burning Tree takes the two scalps and walks slowly toward his mother's burial place. There, in the consciousness of life and death, he buries the scalps alongside his mother's grave.

REVIEW OF THE ANECDOTE

1. What emotions did Burning Tree express upon hearing about the death of his mother?
2. What process did Burning Tree use to go from an unpleasant incident to a state of forgiveness?
3. What is the process you currently use to forgive someone? Does it work successfully for you?
4. What are the three key emotions that prevent someone from expressing forgiveness?
5. How would you respond if someone did something harmful to your loved ones or to you?

Suggestions for Expressing Pure Love

1. Perceive others without societal labels of skin color and beauty.
2. Empower your mind to trust yourself in all your interactions with other people.
3. Empower yourself to see beyond the words spoken by others.
4. Empower your mind to become free of judgment of others.
5. Give freely to children that you don't know.
6. Give freely to individuals who are temporarily deprived of the necessities of life.
7. Empower your mind to understand the meaning of "It is better to give than to receive."
8. Forgive those who have done things to you that have caused you to embrace pain and anger.
9. Love the saint and the murderer equally.
10. Love those family members (children, parents, etc.) who have disappointed you with their actions the same as you love those who have brought you joy.

Seeds from the Ashes

Chapter Five

Peace

You have to first attain peace in your life before you can recognize it in someone else's life.

The cornerstone for achieving empowerment is based on the four-step empowerment solutions program. You can use the four steps Vision, Embodiment, Acceptance, and Action to change the way you think, act, work, and live. For this program to work for you, you must have an open mind and burning desires.

The four-step empowerment solutions program is guaranteed to provide you with results that will lead you to the source of your inner power. The four steps are basic tools, so don't expect them to produce magical results. Nevertheless, if you use them properly, you can discover the great power you have buried beneath the illusions that cause you to doubt yourself.

The four key points to assist you with your search are:

1. Vision: This is the stage of development where you sit quietly with yourself and imagine what you want to express in your life. It takes some time to form a vision that is free of lack, limitation, struggle, doubts, and thoughts of unworthiness. This means you must continue to clear your thoughts so that you are able to perceive yourself with the power to express your greatness. After practicing visioning for several weeks, you will discover that a clear vision does not include victim pleas for jobs, money, and other worldly desires that keep you tied to the illusions. Your vision must be clear and complete in every aspect. You must clear your mind of all the doubts and fears and clearly see yourself existing as the person in your vision. In other words, you see yourself transformed into the new person at the moment of conception rather than at a future date.

2. Embodiment: After you have created a clear vision of yourself existing with power in the present moment, you must assume the identity and behavior of the new person. You must immediately act as if you are what you have envisioned yourself as being or have what you have envisioned yourself as having. Some people find this difficult to do, because after they envision themselves with power, they become mesmerized by the illusions of lack, limitation, and struggle around them. Embodiment is similar to the way an artist acts when he or she has envisioned a great painting. You first clearly envision the work, accept it as so, and then begin the work to express it in the visible world.

3. *Acceptance:* You accept yourself as the source of your power. You and the intuitive power within your mind created the vision of yourself with power. This recognition and acceptance of yourself with power is what you need to nurture your idea through the necessary time interval between conception of the vision and its expression in the visible world. It is during this time interval that you must overcome your previous behavior. The time interval is where you empower your mind to overcome the deleterious habits that cause you to become victimized by lack, limitation, fear, doubt, and struggle. It is also where you must find the power to overcome your dependency on relatives, friends, parents, teachers, and others as your primary support system. This is the time for you to have confidence in yourself. This newfound confidence will empower you to overcome any resistance you might encounter from friends and loved ones in expressing your vision of empowerment.

4. *Action:* All change requires action. It takes action on your part to form a vision of empowerment, embody the vision, and nurture it through the necessary time interval. You must develop a daily action plan to work on your vision of empowerment. This means that you focus all your actions on the work you need to transform yourself into a new person. The challenge here is not to become sidetracked or distracted by other people's actions. You must remain confident that every decision you make is part of the

building process to create a new person.

The four-step empowerment solutions program is a guide to assist you with changing the way you think, act, work, and live. When you accomplish the four steps, this doesn't mean that you have achieved empowerment. It simply means that you have achieved a higher level of awareness than you had before you began to work on yourself.

When you go to a higher level of awareness, there is a tendency to believe you have attained your goal of empowerment rather than accepting the new consciousness as a step on the journey toward achieving your life's goal. The higher you raise your awareness, the better you will feel about using your power to create a successful and empowered lifestyle.

Now that you have an understanding of the four-step empowerment solutions program, you can explore other opportunities that will bring you a step closer to your life's goal. The next step on your journey to achieve empowerment, your life's goal, is to remove the worry and fear from your mind and replace them with a peaceful, unfretted mind. So today, as it was yesterday and as it will be tomorrow, you are required to face your challenges as an empowered warrior.

Today, depending on how you feel, you might believe that a peaceful mind is a fanciful idea. Perhaps you feel this way because it's difficult to express peaceful actions when you are working or interacting with individuals whose actions are disturbing to you.

You might feel that your most peaceful moments seem to happen when you are alone. Moreover, you might believe it is impossible to maintain your peace around people whose actions cause you pain and anger.

There's no getting around the fact that if you want to go to a higher level of awareness, you must learn how to maintain your peace when you interact with other people. You must not allow yourself to get caught up in their energies and behavior. In other words, you must take the high ground rather than wallowing in the mud of anger, suffering, frustration, and pain.

To go to a higher level of awareness, you must know that peace is an expression of unconditional love. The power to express unconditional love means you have the power to live a peaceful life. Achieving a peaceful life will take you some time. This is not something you can do overnight. It takes discipline, vision, and commitment to the empowerment process for you to overcome the illusions in your life.

A mind controlled by illusions is one consumed by someone else's beliefs. The darkness of another individual's beliefs is the foundation for victim consciousness. When you accept someone else's beliefs, it's difficult for you to clearly see other possibilities. If you cannot see other possibilities, then you cannot take action to change your life.

To create other possibilities in your life and achieve peace, one of the first things to do is to expand your ability to think beyond your present limitations. This desire alone will introduce new thoughts and ideas into your life. The objective here is for you to become comfortable with your new thoughts and ideas. You must treat them as real-life beings that you talk and listen to.

The following exchange is an example of what I mean:

ANECDOTE FOR ACHIEVING PEACE

I focus my thoughts in the intuitive time continuum and become one with the humans living in Africa in 1601 A.D. I can almost feel the scorching heat burning my thoughts. There among the thousands of Africans is Udoka, a hardworking, peaceful thirty-one-year-old man with four wives and eight children. He and his family are farmers living in Mali.

Udoka and his family are trying to shield themselves from the scorching heat by lying down in their cozy hut. They look outside at the steamy heat burning everything in sight. They sigh dejectedly, knowing it hasn't rained for months and their crops are dying. To make the situation worse, his children are hungry and his four wives, Chizorah, Kadisha, Saudah, and Kawana, are frustrated and angry.

"What are we going do?" Chizorah shouts. Udoka remains silent. Chizorah shrugs her shoulders and gestures toward the sky and says, "Look, Udoka, we have got to leave this place before we all die. Our crops are already gone. Before long, the same will happen to us if we don't leave here now."

"Ah, c'mon, Chizorah," Udoka says. "You are my first wife. You must set an example for the rest of the family. Anyway, our ancestors will send us the rain. Don't worry!"

"Uh, I don't know, Udoka," Chizorah stammers. "I don't know."

What do you mean you don't know?" Udoka asks.

"I mean, you know—"

"What?"

"The ancestors seem to have forgotten us," Chizorah pleads.

"No, never," Udoka says. "If we maintain faith in the ancestors, I know the rain will come soon. Trust me."

"I do, but I'm scared."

"Don't worry, Chizorah," Udoka assures her. "I won't let anything happen to my family. I trust the ancestors."

"But what if you're wrong?" Chizorah pleads. "What if you're wrong? We will all die."

"Stop that nonsense, woman," Udoka shouts. "I am so sure that it's going to rain that I have begun to dig wells to harness the water. Just wait. You'll see what I mean."

Early the next morning, shortly before dawn, Udoka rises with a new determination to finish the wells before the rains come. He quickly eats the leftovers from last night and gathers his tools to begin the arduous task of digging wells.

He lays his tools on the ground and kneels down to pray to the ancestors, particularly those who had been "keepers of the soil." After several minutes of praying, he takes his tools and begins to dig several large wells several yards from his home. He works all day on digging the wells, only stopping briefly to eat lunch and drink water. He is exhausted at the end of the day; however, as he looks at the nearly finished well, his exhaustion becomes the strength he needs to help him dig the other wells.

After six weeks of continuous digging, Chizorah approaches Udoka as he takes a break from his digging. She once again pleads with him to give up. He continues to ignore her. His other wives, Kadisha, Saudah, and Kawana, join with Chizorah in pleading with him to stop digging the empty wells. He admonishes them to accept his role as head of the family, which they do.

Six weeks later, several of Udoka's male friends, who had packed up and left nearly a month ago, come back to the village to plead with him to leave.

"You have to give this up, Udoka," his friend Mutumwa pleads. "I know that you are a strong, determined, and peaceful man, but we think it's time to stop digging these empty wells. You have to take your family away from this desolate place as soon as you can."

"He's telling you the truth," another friend, Manu, says. "The entire village has been destroyed by the spirits you're praying to."

"That's the truth, my friend," Mutumwa says, raising his hands toward the sun. It's over, Udoka. It's time to go."

"I'm not afraid," Udoka says. "I am beyond worrying about

the future. I live in this moment of time. It is either a good time or a bad time based upon my faith. I submitted my life to the ancestors, and they have given me peace. I don't need rain to give me peace"

"Why not?" Mutumwa interrupts.

"Because peace is what liberates you from worry. You see, Mutumwa, when worry is present in your life, peace is overlooked."

"What do you mean?"

"Peace is present in every moment, every circumstance, and every life until someone challenges it with doubt and worry."

"What are you talking about, man?" Mutumwa asks. "Has the sun made you mad?"

"No, Mutumwa, I'm not mad," Udoka chuckles. "Far from it. Look around you."

"For what?" Mutumwa mumbles. "There's nothing to see."

"Oh yes, there's plenty to see. Look at the scorching heat and arid soil. They are not fighting with each other. One is not worried that the other needs to disappear before its time. They remain connected by their divine purpose in a peaceful and harmonious cycle of life."

"Okay," Manu says. "Fine. But tell me, my brother, how is this going to feed your family?"

"It is my faith and conviction in the power of the unknown that will feed my family," Udoka says confidently. "I will remain resolute in my convictions until the rain appears and confirms what I already know is true. Then you will see the fruits of my labor rise from beneath the fears, doubts, and worries."

Mutumwa and Manu raise their hands in a gesture of despair, mumbling to themselves as they bid Udoka farewell. Udoka thanks them for their concerns and continues to dig, determined to finish the seventh and last well.

After digging all day, he finally finishes the seventh well exactly seven months after he began digging the wells. As he wipes the sweat from his brow, he looks up momentarily at the clear blue sky and smiles. He has overcome the doubters and naysayers. He is able to stand alone and basks in his victory of completing the wells in such a short period of time. His throat lumps with unimaginable joy while he stares blankly at the seven wells.

As his eyes examine the wells one by one, he notices how each one is created in a perfect circle. The perfection of the wells seems almost surreal because he had no instruments with which to measure them. Yet there they are, perfect. Udoka pauses for a moment as he ponders how it happened. "It must have been the ancestors," he says to himself.

Udoka turns away from the wells and watches as the sun disappears to prepare for the moon and stars to light up the sky. He chuckles as he watches the moon rise slowly into the darkness and take its place among the stars. As Udoka basks in the coolness of the moment, the clouds grow dark and lighting strikes a menacing pose against the dark sky.

A few minutes later, he feels several raindrops fall against his baked skin. He laughs loudly as the rain begins to pour down from the skies. "Thank you, Ancestors," he shouts.

His wives and children peer out at the rain from the open window. They embrace each other with hugs and kisses. Overcome with joy, with teary eyes and running noses, they run toward Udoka. Udoka hears their laughter and cheers as he turns and sees them running to him. He greets them with powerful hugs and welcomes their love and affection. His family continues to shower him with undying love for several minutes. Overcome with gratitude, Udoka stands helpless in a utopian moment of family bliss. There is nothing for him to say or do but accept their gifts of love.

After nearly an hour of family celebration, Udoka asks his family to be silent because he wants to name the wells. He turns toward the wells, extends his arms high above his head, and says, "I shall name these seven wells the *Wells of Peace*, because they brought peace to my household."

Udoka and his family continue to celebrate as the rain pours down heavy streams of water upon the land. Udoka interrupts the celebration long enough to say, "The peace and joy you feel now was available for you to have before the rains came. I want you to remember this feeling after the rain disappears and the hot sun returns."

Everyone remains silent, listening to the rain and Udoka's voice. The rain continues for twenty-eight days, overflowing the wells with water. Udoka's family uses the water to nourish their crops. They also share their wealth with their friends and neighbors who returned with the rain.

On the seventh day, after the rains stop, Udoka invites everyone in the village to a community-style get-together. The wives prepare wonderful food dishes, while the children run and play near the men, who enjoy their drinks and the laughter among themselves. Udoka watches all this with a deep sense of commitment and peace of mind. He is happy because his family and friends are here with him to share this moment.

Udoka turns and walks to the center of the group and says, "My family and I welcome all of you here as our friends. I know that life is good. Everyone is happy once again. Let's not forget that this moment is here because of our ancestors. They deserve the credit for guiding us through the drought."

Everyone applauds Udoka. They shout his name over and over again. He is their hero, the one who never doubted that it would rain and who maintained his peace when others around him pleaded with him to give up his quest for rain.

REVIEW OF THE ANECDOTE

1. What emotions did Udoka express when everyone around him complained about the hot weather and lack of rain?
2. What actions did Udoka take to go beyond the doubters to his level of activity?
3. What is the process you currently use to live a peaceful life? Does it work successfully for you?
4. What are the three key emotions that prevent someone from expressing peace?
5. How would you respond if your family and friends doubted your abilities to overcome a serious problem?

Suggestions for Expressing Peace in All Your Actions

1. Begin your day with at least thirty minutes of quiet meditation.
2. Empower your mind to remain still and focused in joyful and sorrowful situations.
3. Empower yourself to trust the intuitive-empowerment process.
4. Trust yourself to remain empowered when you're in the presence of dysfunctional activities.
5. Respond to others who commit acts of aggression toward you in a kind, humble, and empowered manner.
6. Remain empowered wherever you are and in whatever circumstances you are in.
7. Forgive those who have said things about you that hurt you deeply.
8. Empower yourself to remain peaceful when you go to sleep and when you arise the next day.
9. Empower your mind to begin your day with a vision of empowerment.
10. Empower yourself to refrain from gossip about others (politicians, leaders, coworkers, supervisors, relatives, friends, and enemies).

Chapter Six

Wisdom

When you discover the wisdom hidden in your mind, you will know the truth about yourself.

A troublesome obstacle you face in changing your life is the belief you have about your present level of intelligence. Most individuals that are unhappy with their lives believe it is because they're not smart enough to change it.

Many victims believe you can only achieve success by being smarter or intellectually superior to others. So if you find yourself without a college degree, you might feel intellectually inferior to people with degrees. The more you empower them, the more you disempower yourself.

For most people in this country, knowledge and education are considered synonymous with success and wealth. A graduate of a prestigious university is expected to be happy and successful in his or her career. A high school graduate is expected to be happy with a mediocre career, while a high school dropout is expected to be unhappy with his or her life. Like it or not, we measure people's intelligence and capabilities to succeed in life by their level of education.

Most poor and middle-income people with little formal education find it difficult to create many options in their lives. Unfortunately for them, it means they must accept jobs that require very few skills, which means they must work for the *smart* people. Regardless of where you are intellectually and academically, you must believe and know that you have the power to change the way you think and live. The confidence you give yourself comes from the inner wisdom that teaches you that there is a major distinction between education and wisdom: Education is measured by your knowledge about other people, places, and things, while wisdom is measured by the knowledge you have about your unconditional inner power. Moreover, it is wisdom that opens your mind to see beyond the limitations of education.

To have confidence in your decision-making ability, you first must acknowledge that you are naturally intelligent, smart, and wise. To think of yourself as being less than this would mean that you are inadequate to achieve success and empowerment. To think of yourself as already possessing the inner wisdom to be successful does not mean that you do not have to learn about other people, places, and things. It simply means that you will use this additional information to enhance the beliefs you have about your own power.

To say or think that you are exceptionally intelligent, smart, and wise only requires a simple thought from your mind. This thought about who you are and your level of intelligence is all that is required to begin the process of changing the way you think, act, work, and live. The power of your thoughts is what creates the changes in your life.

Every idea expressed throughout the universe comes from a single thought. It is the source of all life forms, visible and invisible. This thought comes from an omniscient consciousness. It has no barriers to its expression. To recognize that you are a part of this thought, you must overcome the illusions that victimize you and cause you to devalue yourself.

The moment you enter your thoughts into the oneness with this single thought of creation, you immediately see the seven lights of empowerment. From that moment and until the end of all moments, you know that there are no other thoughts. All that can ever be conceptualized and expressed in your life is contained in this thought. It is this awareness and acceptance of yourself as being a part of this power that will empower you to feel good about yourself right now.

The truth about yourself is found in the wisdom of your unrestrictive intuitive consciousness. From this consciousness you are able to express your ideas without fears, doubts, and limitations. When you trust this decision-making process, you free your mind of the self-imposed illusions causing the pain and suffering in your life.

If you take a moment to examine what you think of yourself right now, you will clearly know that the illusions in your life come from your knowledge about other people, places, and things. This knowledge about the world is what keeps you tied to victim beliefs. As a victim-thinking person, you abdicate your power to others and admire their accomplishments.

Whenever you allow your thoughts to become victimized by illusions, you lose sight of your power to use the great wisdom in your mind. This type of thinking diminishes you to thinking like a victim and perceiving all greatness as occurring outside of yourself. From this level of awareness, you observe others expressing their greatness on television, in the movies, or at sports events and wish you had the power to do what they're doing.

When you feel lowly and inadequate, it is easy to confuse someone else's success with your own. What you observe others accomplishing in life has little to do with you and the great treasure of greatness buried deep in your mind. Sometimes it is easy to forget that there is no treasure to find without a seeker. For you, your treasure of wisdom is found within your mind. Fortunately, you have the opportunity to use it to change your life.

To move forward in your search for wisdom, you first must

clear your thoughts so that you feel the freedom to think beyond your present limitations. Then you must act as if you already have the wisdom and knowledge to change the way you think and live. The following anecdote is an example to assist you with thinking beyond your current limitations and doubts.

ANECDOTE FOR ACHIEVING WISDOM

As I relax and close my eyes to the illusions around me, I suddenly feel my thoughts expanding with clarity. I am imagining myself going to a higher level of consciousness where I have clarity of purpose about my power. This clarity allows me to understand what it feels like to think creatively.

"Well, Advocate, how do you feel?" Wisdom asks, interrupting my thoughts.

"Like a child taking my first step. I feel wonderful."

"Good! Now let's change past time to present time."

I watch as the yesterdays pass through my mind and become one with my level of awareness. The silhouettes of past lives suddenly become alive once again in my thoughts during the time period 3000 B.C.

I watch as the pyramids are being built in Egypt. The world is flourishing with knowledge and unprecedented energy. I focus my thoughts on the vibrant city of Thebes and a man, Atum, known throughout the country for his love of wisdom. Unfortunately, most of his neighbors and friends don't share his passion for wisdom.

They believe he is an odd man driven by eccentric desires. He is one of the individuals who eschew the Egyptians' love for mathematics and science in favor of what he refers to as the love of intuitive wisdom. Most Egyptians refuse to talk to him.

Atum shares his wisdom about the origin of life with anyone willing to listen. On this particular day, he is sitting alone near the marketplace when Menekama and his son, Wose, approach him. Menekama greets Atum and says, "Is it true what they say about you?"

"Yes, it is true," Atum chuckles.

"But—you don't know what I'm about to ask you?"

"Yes, I do."

"What?"

"Am I a lover of wisdom?"

"That's right! How did you know?"

"Well, my friend, that's difficult to explain," Atum says, shrugging his shoulders. "I know you want something from me and all that I have is wisdom. So what can I do for you and your son?"

"But sir, I do seek wisdom," Menekama says. "That's why I am here seeking it from you. Well, actually, I am seeking it for my son. I want you to teach him wisdom."

"Why do you want him to have wisdom?"

"Because everyone in the community considers him an idiot, a moron. But if you can teach him wisdom, they will respect him and me. I also am tired of being ridiculed by friends and neighbors as being the father of an idiot."

"I beg you, kind sir, let the boy speak to me," Atum says.

"Tell me, boy, what is it that you seek from me?"

"Uh, sir, I am Wose and I seek wisdom," Wose stutters. "I want wisdom so that my father will be proud of me and the other children will stop calling me an idiot."

"Very well," Atum says. "I will teach you how to achieve wisdom; however, you must remember that this is a private journey. You cannot take your father with you."

"Yes sir, I understand," Wose says as he turns and bids his father goodbye.

"Good! Now tell me: Do you remember the first time someone called you an idiot?"

"Yes sir," Wose chuckles. "It was my father."

"Your father?"

"Yes sir, he called me an idiot because I wasn't as smart as my four brothers. Shortly after that, my mother began calling me an idiot. Then my four brothers joined my parents in calling me an idiot. After months of calling me an idiot in our home, my brothers began calling me an idiot at school and around my friends and classmates. It didn't take long before everyone at school called me an idiot."

"How did you feel when they called you an idiot?"

"I felt like I thought an idiot was supposed to feel," Wose

says. "I mean, I actually became an idiot in my mind to please my parents."

"Why?"

"Because I thought an idiot was a special person, someone my father talked to his friends about all the time.

"What do you mean?"

"Well, I used to hear my father say to his friends, 'Now, this boy, Wose, he's an idiot. He's not like my other four boys. You know, he's the first idiot in our family.' That's when I wanted know what an idiot was. I wanted to know who created me."

"Very good, Wose," Atum says, complimenting the boy for his insights. "Did you find this knowledge?"

"Yes, I found it. It was right there in front of me."

"What do you mean?"

"It was my father, Menekama. He is the creator of an idiot. I know this because when I began my search, I discovered that the knowledge that created all of us did not create any idiots."

"How do you know this?"

"Well, everyone calls you an idiot, and you refer to yourself as wisdom. So there is something within your mind that reminds you that you're not an idiot. I believe that *something* has to be wisdom or you would have accepted yourself the way everyone in the city describes you."

"So true, Wose, so true," Atum says, placing his arm around Wose's shoulder in a fatherly gesture. "I know that I am wisdom because I am greater than everything I see and hear in this world. I am greater because I know that I existed before the world was created—"

"Uh, how do you know this?"

"I know it because I see wisdom present in you and your father and everyone I meet. It's there beneath the layers of human confusion and illusions. I accept human ridicule because I know the source of the ridicule—"

"But—what is the source?" Wose asks.

"Look, Wose, the source is all around you. Look at the great pyramids. Look at the powerful physicians, the priests, the teachers and politicians. They are the source of all human ridicule, because they believe wisdom is found only in their creations.

"Don't you agree?"

"No! I know that I am wisdom, not the things I see in the world," Atum says. "Wisdom, pure wisdom, exists in its purest form only when you see beyond your limitations."

"Is this what gives you confidence?" Wose asks.

"Yes," Atum says, "it allows me to say that I am wisdom. So whenever someone calls me an idiot, I pay no attention to them because I know that I am a wise man."

"Thank you, Mr. Atum," Wose says. "Now I can tell my father that I have achieved wisdom—"

"Well, at least you can tell him you know where to find wisdom," Atum says, embracing Wose with a fatherly hug. "Have an empowered day, Wose."

Atum waves as Wose heads home to tell his father the good news. Wose rushes into the house to tell his father that he is no longer an idiot. His new name is Wisdom. Menekama embraces his son and calls his wife and other sons into the room and says, "I want you to know that Wose is no longer an idiot. He has found wisdom. So none of you should ever refer to him as an idiot again. He is wisdom."

This anecdote is an exercise to remind you to never accept what others say about you.

REVIEW OF THE ANECDOTE

1. What emotions did Wose express about his father believing he was an idiot?
2. What process did Wose use to go from thinking of himself as an idiot to thinking of himself as smart or wise?
3. What is the process you currently use to overcome aspersions about your intelligence or competency? Does it work successfully for you?
4. What are the three key emotions that prevent someone from perceiving himself or herself as intelligent?
5. How would you respond if someone labeled you as an idiot or dumb?

Suggestions for Expressing Wisdom in All Your Actions

1. Empower your mind to find the vast knowledge about yourself hidden in your intuitive-empowered consciousness.
2. Train your thoughts to deter all detrimental information from entering into your consciousness.
3. Learn the difference between wisdom and knowledge.
4. Use your wisdom to overcome the illusions in your life.
5. Share your wisdom with others freely and without restrictions.
6. Condition your thoughts to produce ideas that will give you success and empowerment.
7. Develop the discipline to meditate and relax your thoughts several times each day.
8. Use your wisdom to discover your purpose for being in human form.
9. Allow your wisdom to guide you in all your daily activities.
10. Use your wisdom to create a plan to change the way you think, act, work, and live.

Chapter Seven
Freedom

The expression of a thought is the greatest freedom of all.

The desire to be free of a relentless, suffocating life filled with failure and setbacks is a powerful feeling. Yet you feel like this when the pain and suffering overwhelm you to the point where you must seek an immediate solution to change how you think and live. All that it takes to jettison your brain cells into a swirl of creativity is to decide to change the way you think and live. From this moment forward, you will focus only on freeing your mind to search for the limitless possibilities available to you. This is the journey you make on the way to freedom.

Whenever you think of freedom, you think of empowerment. Whenever you think of empowerment, you stop thinking of yourself as a victim. One of the greatest stumbling blocks on the road to empowerment is losing one's life to an illusion. To lose your life to an illusion is to admit failure. And anyone who accepts failure knows he or she will not overcome victim beliefs anytime soon. When you become a slave to one illusion, you become a slave to all illusions. As a slave, you obey your master—the illusions of lack, limitation, and struggle—because it seems easier to accept yourself as a slave than as a master. Anyone who thinks like a slave knows how to live a mediocre life. Nevertheless, the choice to express greatness or accept mediocrity is always available to you. The mind, however, must be conditioned to emancipate itself from thinking like a victim before you can change how you think and live.

The decision to accept mediocrity as a life goal is not a lofty one, nor is it one that, over time, makes you feel good about yourself. Those individuals that choose to live mediocre lives are usually unaware they are living in this manner. Nevertheless, that's what you are doing when you accept less than what is rightfully yours.

The moment you realize you are living a mediocre life is the moment you feel the intense pain and suffering anchoring you in a sea of failure. For many individuals, the idea of failure and its ramifications of defining one as a victim are difficult to accept. For you to reach this level of acknowledgment, the pain and suffering are usually very intense. And whatever you think about your life, you know clearly that you must do something different to change the way you think and live.

For anyone who feels like a victim, whether he or she acknowledges it or not, it always appears easier to remain where you are than to empower your mind to create a goal of success. The journey to overcome a mediocre lifestyle requires you to think outside your current limitations. You must swim further away from your problems until you go beyond their influence. The further you go, the clearer your vision of success and empowerment will become to you.

Today, because of how you are feeling, you might desire to change your life. You might also believe that you can do this only by seeking help from outside sources. This is something all victims must undergo to free their minds. Part of thinking like a victim is acknowledging your dependency on other people and their beliefs. The goal of freeing your mind requires you to trust your inner thoughts to guide you to empowerment.

As you know, it is very difficult to trust your inner thoughts. And with any process to change your life, you must remain committed to your new goal until it expresses itself in your life. This means you cannot abandon your work because you don't see visible results right away. This is easier said than done. It is inevitable for most people to abandon their inner journey temporarily to seek assistance from other people or from a higher religious power.

For you to seek religious support is not good or bad, nor right or wrong. In moments of great despair, when your esteem is low, you will undoubtedly turn to religion to assist you with solving the seemingly insoluble problems in your life. When the pain in your life becomes unbearable, you will try just about anything to help free yourself from it. Since religion is an acceptable source of power to assist those with seemingly insoluble problems, it is what many people use to overcome their problems.

The point here is not for you to rely solely on religion so that you don't take the necessary action to solve your own problems. Religion is just one source for you to use. There are many others. The bottom line is: your problems must be solved by the actions you take. Where you get the inspiration and motivation to act is not as important as the actions.

The freedom to think means you have the power to act. The problems in your life were created by your actions and your actions alone. This means you cannot turn them over to religion or someone else to solve them for you.

When you create outcomes in your life that you don't particularly like, you must accept the responsibility for your behavior. Why ask Jesus Christ, Mohammed, Buddha, Confucius, or any other deity to solve your problems when you have the power to solve them yourself? The power you give to someone else must also be present in you. If you perceive others to be greater than you, then how do you perceive yourself? For you to think of yourself as being less than someone else is to demean and belittle your own great power. In other words, you burglarize your own power and give it to someone else. This type of thinking reduces you to a common burglar who robs yourself of power in order to please others.

To search for a great power somewhere in the sky or from another individual is to deny that you have the power within your mind to solve your problems. The freedom to think beyond societal restrictions is not found in an abstract, unknown universe, but in your mind.

One method to use to free your mind of restrictive thoughts is meditation, prayer, or visualization. While you are in a prayer-meditative state of consciousness it is easy to envision yourself as a colorless, faceless, and formless being. When you remove the limitations of color and form from your life, you open your mind to go beyond the illusions creating all the pain and suffering in your life.

Remember: when you pray, you are seeking a solution to your problem from a higher source, which must respond in such a way that your mind can receive and interpret the answer. If you write on paper the dialogue occurring in your prayers, it might assist you with understanding that everything you say and do is occurring in your mind.

ANECDOTE FOR ACHIEVING FREEDOM

You can travel effortlessly in your mind by imagining that you are free of time restrictions. This is something you do quite frequently when you recall something that happened in the past. When you free your mind of all time restrictions, you can travel to any time period you choose. For example, you can imagine you are present during 1944, shortly before the end of World War II. This will allow you to observe the feelings and experiences of a family living in Auschwitz, a German concentration camp.

Let's imagine that you focus on one particular family, the Rubensteins, which consists of Jacob and Ruth and their sons, Aaron and Joseph. The Rubensteins are devout practitioners of the Jewish faith. Although Jacob and his family are devout members of Judaism, as prisoners it is difficult for them to practice their religion. The restrictions of prison have caused Jacob to reevaluate his faith.

Before Hitler's rise to power in 1933, Jacob was a successful businessman. On a springtime day in May 1944, the German soldiers come suddenly to forcibly remove him and his family from their home. They beat Jacob, curse his wife and children, handcuff them, and pile them like animals onto the cold cattle car, along with nearly a hundred other Jews. Jacob almost suffocates when he smells the urine, feces, and dried blood permeating the air. He quickly covers his nose and mouth with his hand as he takes his place alongside the other prisoners.

Jacob remembers the pride he felt about being named after the patriarch Jacob in the Bible. And now, like the Biblical Jacob, he has lost all of his wealth, property, and freedom to worship God. It pains him to think about his life now compared to what it was a few years ago.

Jacob closes his eyes for a few moments in a hopeless attempt to erase this nightmare from his mind. When he opens them, everything is still the same; he and his family are prisoners headed to an unknown destination, which frightens him. He had prayed that his nightmare would disappear and he would be safe at home with his family. Now he knows that he is a prisoner, and he can only imagine what the Nazis are going to do to him and the other prisoners.

After traveling for most of the day and night, Jacob and the other prisoners arrive at the concentration camp, where they are greeted with curses and blows to their bodies. They are shackled and beaten and their bloodied bodies dragged into the barracks-like buildings, where they are strip-searched and humiliated by the guards.

Jacob stares helplessly as the male German guards search and fondle his wife and the other women. With each touch, he feels a part of himself die. The deep anger within him fights to be heard, but he knows he must freeze his anger and thaw it out later.

After an hour or more of enduring unthinkable humiliation, degradation, and torture, it is finally over. The guards order them

Seeds from the Ashes

to line up against the wall and to march single file toward another barracks about fifty yards away.

When they arrive at the barracks, Jacob is dead tired and ready to get some rest. He comforts his family and gets them settled, and then he falls exhausted onto the bed. "Rest, finally," Jacob sighs.

Shortly after he lies down, the guards return. They take him and his family to another building filled with emaciated-looking men, women, and children lining up to get their prisoner identification. One after another, Jacob watches and listens to screams and shouts from the prisoners each time the guards use a hot branding iron to burn a number on their arm.

When the torture is finally over, the guards take Jacob and the other prisoners back to their barracks. During the walk back, Jacob thinks about his new life as a prisoner and what impact it will have on him and his family. He begins to think of Yahweh and his commitment to his religious faith.

As he dwells on his life, he asks himself: "Will the guards permit us to practice our religion? Can we pray? How important is my religion? Is it worth dying for?" Questions and more questions are all that he can form now, because he has no answers. He only knows as he limps, exhausted, in a drugged-out state of mind toward his new home that the number branded on his arm makes him a German prisoner.

When they arrive at the barracks, the guards curse them and

Freedom

order them to clean up the place. As they walk away, Jacob stares at them until they are out of sight, then he turns to his family and says, "Don't worry, everything is going to be all right. You'll see."

"I hope so," Ruth sighs, placing her arms around her children. "I hope so."

Jacob sits down slowly on the bed and begins to think about his religious faith. According to his religious beliefs, he and his family are exempt from observing mitzvoth (commandments) because they are prisoners and their lives are endangered. Nonetheless, Jacob believes that he and his family must continue to observe the mitzvoth in spite of the inherent dangers. For him, keeping the mitzvoth is a form of resistance against German oppression. He believes it is a way for his family and him to maintain their spiritual freedom while in prison.

Jacob takes his wife's hand and asks his sons to clasp hands and join them in prayer. They take each other's hands and kneel down to pray. After a few moments of silent meditation, their prayer is interrupted by loud, menacing voices.

"Get off your knees, you Jew pigs," shouts the German officer.

"How dare you pray in the presence of a German officer—"

"But—Sir, I thought—"

"Silence, pig!" the officer shouts, striking Jacob in the head with the butt of his rifle. The blow stuns Jacob momentarily, causing him to see tiny stars twinkling around him as he struggles to stand. He reaches for his head and feels a warm, wet substance flowing down the side of his face. Without thinking, he touches it with his right hand and sees that it's blood, his blood, which sends him into temporary shock. "My God, am I going to die now?" he asks himself.

The German officer stands over him and says, "Don't ever interrupt me, you Jew swine. Wait until I tell you to speak."

"Yes sir," Jacob says, continuing to wipe the blood from the side of his face and hair.

"That's better," the officer says with a smug arrogance.

Ruth stares in horror and disbelief as Jacob wipes the blood from his head and face. She rushes toward him and shouts, "Jacob! Jacob! Jacob, are you all right? Jacob—"

"Shut up, you Jew whore," the German officer shouts. "If you take another step, I'll blow the Jew bastard's head off. "
Ruth stops immediately, drops to her knees, and pleads, "Please sir, don't kill my husband. He's a good man. He won't cause you any—"

"I thought I told you to shut up, you Jew bitch," the German officer shouts. "Silence, that's all I want to hear from you Jew swine."

Ruth remains silent. She can only think of the impending death of her husband and perhaps of herself and her family, too. She suddenly thinks of her faith in God and begins to silently pray to God to protect her family. She asks God to deliver her from the hands of her enemies, to keep the promise he made to her ancestors thousands of years ago.

Several moments later, the German officer grabs Jacob by his neck and says, "Get up, you Jew bastard." He squeezes his hands tighter around Jacob's neck, lifts him up, and pushes him toward Ruth, who is now sobbing. Jacob and Ruth embrace momentarily for what seems like an eternity. Jacob takes her hand and walks over to rejoin their two sobbing sons, who have watched the entire event.

"Are you all right, father?" Aaron asks, taking his father's hand. He helps him to sit down and offers him comfort by wiping the blood from his hair and face.

The younger son, Joseph, embraces his father and mother and whispers to his father, "Don't worry, father, God will deliver us from this place just like he did for our ancestors."

Jacob embraces his sons with moist eyes, struggling to hold back the tears. He knows that he must demonstrate strength to his sons. He also knows that it is God's love for him and his family that has spared their lives so far. And unless he gains his freedom soon, he doesn't know what will happen to them.

Jacob sits quietly for a few moments. His thoughts focus only on obtaining his freedom. That's when he sees his good friend Abe Saberstein talking with a couple of prisoners. Abe walks over to Jacob, places his hand on his shoulder, and says, "Don't worry, my friend, your head wound will heal. However, it is your mind and spirit that you must keep healthy. Fortunately for all of us, we have a very strong rabbi here. You know him—"

"You don't mean—"

"Yes, Rabbi Farbenstein is here. He arrived several weeks ago."

"That's great news. I need to talk with him right away."

"Hold on, my friend, we must proceed cautiously or they might kill him and all of us too, if we're not careful. As you probably can imagine by now, the Germans won't allow us to congregate. So we have devised a communication system that allows us to disseminate information by word of mouth."

"Very good," Jacob says. "But what about religious services? What are we going to do about that?"

"Well, " Abe says, "several of the men met with the rabbi a couple of days ago to discuss our religious obligations toward practicing our faith during our imprisonment. He told us to remain committed to mitzvoth regardless of the circumstances. He also said that in order to save our lives we can eat chametz."

"I hope it doesn't come to that," Jacob says.

"I know," Abe says. "However, he also said that in the meantime, we will eat matzah and adhere to mitzvoth. He said each one of us must pray daily and ask God to send us a Deliverer to get us out of this hellhole."

"Okay, my friend," Jacob says, patting Abe on the back. "I will pray to God and ask him for guidance. I'll ask my sons and wife to pray, too."

Freedom

Jacob bids Abe goodbye. He immediately begins to pray to God for guidance. He prays daily for several weeks without noticing any changes in his life or the lives of the other prisoners. One night, when everyone is asleep, Jacob is suddenly awakened by a hot, burning sensation on his forehead. At first, he thinks it is from his head wound, and then he sees a brightly colored plume of smoke covering his face. "What is this?" he mumbles to himself.

"I am the spirit Moses," a voice says. "I am come to deliver you and your family from this place—"

"Uh, but—how?"

"By teaching you how to remove the shackles of dogma and fear that imprison your mind. The freedom you seek is within you. You must learn how to use your mind to create your freedom right here, in the midst of great suffering. Your freedom will come from Heaven, which is within your consciousness."

"How can I think about Heaven when my family and I are starving to death?"

"It is easy. First you must free your thoughts of all religious beliefs—"

"Uh, wait, you don't mean—"

"I do. Mitzvoth and matzah are merely reflections of the great power within you. The freedom you seek is greater than your commandments and the food you eat."

"I don't know if I can do this," Jacob says. "The mitzvoth and matzah represent our core religious beliefs. If I abandon them, I will no longer be recognized as a Jew."

"Oh yes, you will," the image says. "After you condition your thoughts to express freedom, you will provide the others with the tools to create a new way of life. This new conditioning of the mind will allow all of you to gain your freedom while you are in prison."

"Does this mean my family will live?" Jacob asks.

"Yes, if you achieve the freedom of consciousness before the spirit of death claims them."

"Okay, I want to do it. I'll do anything to save my family."

"No," the image says, "the question is: will you do anything to free your mind to achieve freedom? The consciousness of freedom is greater than your love for your family."

Jacob remains silent, because he knows that what he is being asked to do is a monumental task. Yet he knows that if he wants to free himself and his family, he must learn how to empower his mind to overcome the illusions of being in prison. So he listens as the image of Moses speaks quietly to him about how to create a vision of empowerment to free him from the prison of his beliefs and illusions about who he is.

After several months of visualizing himself as a free person, the image returns and says, "Jacob, I want you to go to your rabbi and tell him it is okay for the people to eat chametz. You must convince him that the God of your ancestors has sent you to him. Tell him the vision of empowerment clearly revealed to you that all the people here must act from a position of empowerment and freedom even when the spirit of death comes for them.

"What is important is how you live, not how you leave your body. When your oppressors see you acting from an empowered position, they will know that the shackles have been removed from your mind and body—"

"Excuse me," Jacob interrupts. "Did you say earlier that my family would be saved from the spirit of death?"

"Yes, and they will," the image says. "They will stay with their bodies. However, you must leave your body soon."

"But why?" Jacob asks. "I have done everything I was asked to do. I have envisioned myself free of this place. I have taught the others to act empowered. I have worked with the rabbi to console the weak and weary."

"That's true," the image says. "Now you must express the purity of freedom. You will not die, because an empowered person never dies."

Jacob is sad momentarily. He watches as the image disappears from his sight. During the next few months and into the next year, Jacob continues to express freedom in all of his daily activities. He teaches and inspires the other prisoners not to submit themselves as slaves to their German captors.

During the early months of 1945, similar to the way it was in the summer of 1944, the spirit of death reigns upon the prisoners, and thousands of Jews are killed each month. However, those prisoners who have been inspired by Jacob's freedom of consciousness vision meet the spirit of death as empowered individuals. Not a single Jew, man, woman, or child, submits themselves to the Germans as slaves. They are all empowered and free in life and death.

During the death camps in 1945, the German soldiers become suspicious of Jacob and his relationship with the other prisoners. They suspect that he was responsible for the way in which the Jews met their deaths. After a few days of deliberation, the Germans decide to publicly kill Jacob in front of the other prisoners. This, they hope, will make the others submit willingly to their leadership over them.

In late March 1945, shortly before the surrender of the German army, several soldiers come for Jacob. The sun is beginning to rise. Jacob looks at the wonderful sight and thinks of the great power that created it. He smiles as he walks willingly with the German officers.

After taking a few steps, Jacob pauses briefly, turns to his friend Abe, and says, "Remember everything I have said and done. They were not my words or deeds, but the power within me. And because I have done these things, because I have expressed freedom, you will now all live."

One of the German officers suddenly punches Jacob in the face with his fist and shouts, "Shut up, you Jew swine. Look at your people for the last time, because you're going to become soap soon. Ha, ha, ha."

As Jacobs walks toward the gravesite, the closer he gets, the more pronounced the odorous smell of dead bodies. He looks at the large, open hole, filled with countless dead bodies, and cringes at the sight of human destruction. He is momentarily stunned, and then up from the ashes of death, he sees the image of Moses shining brightly upon him.

The image moves closer until it completely engulfs Jacobs's body and says, "Jacob, do you feel the freedom and empowerment present in your thoughts?"

"Yes, I do," Jacob says. "I know that I have finished the work that you asked me to do. I know the freedom that I feel now is who I am."

"Who are you talking to?" one of the German officers asks.

"I am talking to myself, that part of me that knows the truth about life and death. It is the same voice my ancestors heard thousands of years ago."

The German officer frowns and says to the other officers, "I told you there's something strange about this Jew. He's not afraid of us or of death. Look at him!"

"Yeah, I see him," one of the officers says. "What do you think he's looking at? You know, he seems to be staring straight ahead and talking to someone."

"Who knows?" the officer says. "Anyway, who cares? Let's get this over with so I can go home to my family."

"Yeah, you're right," the other officer says. "He's just another dirty Jew swine, that's all."

After Jacob has walked several more feet up to the edge of the gravesite, the image of Moses shows him the spirits of all the lifeless bodies lying beneath him and says, "You are already free. Death does not validate your freedom; your life does."

Jacob doesn't hear the gunshot that opens his brain with such force that it catapults his body into the gravesite below. Jacob chuckles as he watches his body fall into the gravesite. He now knows that he is free of his responsibility to accept himself as a human being.

The purpose of this anecdote is to encourage you to go beyond your fixed beliefs and explore other possibilities. When you discover your inner power, you are free to live however you choose.

REVIEW OF THE ANECDOTE

1. What emotions did Jacob express about his family and himself being imprisoned in a German concentration camp?
2. What process did Jacob use to overcome his fears and gain his confidence?
3. What is the process you currently use to overcome your fears? Does it work successfully for you?
4. What are the three key emotions that prevent someone from remaining firmly committed to their vision?
5. How would you respond if someone took away your freedom or the freedom of a loved one?

Suggestions for Expressing Freedom in All Your Actions

1. Empower your mind to go beyond human limitations.
2. Condition your thoughts to move freely in your mind.
3. Use meditation as a vessel of creative energy.
4. Practice daily self-abnegation of those beliefs that imprison your mind.
5. Complete daily creative mind exercises.
6. Envision yourself with limitless power.
7. Remove the beliefs that you have about your worthiness to express the freedom of success and empowerment.
8. Search for the limitless choices to make your decisions.
9. Open your mind to the world of new ideas.
10. Use your freedom of mind to create a plan to change the way you think, act, work, and live.

Chapter Eight
Abundance

A strong belief in yourself will allow you to live life more abundantly.

During your journey on the road to empowerment, there are days when you feel small, insignificant, and powerless in comparison to others. Perhaps, if you are like many people, you feel this way when you are without money, status, and purpose. From this low point in life, there is a tendency for you to envy those with wealth and fame.

Today, the truth about your current status in life is based entirely on your value system. If you value money and fame, you will undoubtedly feel inadequate without them. Moreover, if you change your value system, you change the way you think about your life. You, and you alone, have the power to change your values to whatever you want them to be.

One way to imagine this change is to envision yourself as an integral part of the universe. The universe reflects the Creator's thoughts about you and your status in the world. It confirms to you and to the world that you are alive. The confirmation of your being alive empowers you to exist beyond the illusions of wealth and fame. Once you achieve this level of awareness, you clearly know that for life to be meaningful and purposeful, it must exist without your accepting societal labels regarding your identity. You clearly know that to change the way you think and live, you must perceive yourself existing without limitations to your power.

Nonetheless, there are some days when you just feel inadequate. On those days when you feel restricted and powerless, you must recognize the power you have to create an abundant lifestyle. The thought of abundance comes from the vastness of your mind, which is a part of the universe. This means that both your mind and the universe contain within them the capacity and power for you to live life more abundantly.

It seems to me that when people think about living life more abundantly, they frequently focus on attaining material wealth. Few individuals ever think of focusing on empowering their minds. For many victims, abundance means having a successful career, a great education, and lots of money.

Victims of the illusions spend countless hours watching television and reading books and magazines about the lives of rich and famous people. Many of them believe that if they learn how people become rich and famous, they will also live this way. Many of these victims daydream about becoming rich and famous while their actions produce for them a life of mediocrity. Unfortunately, after achieving mediocrity, they eschew greatness and learn how to live with less.

Nearly every day some media outlets promote people who have achieved billions of dollars. In nearly every instance, they all appear to be happy. The public yearns to see more of them and follows their lives more closely than their own. When a victim sees wealth and prosperity, he or she sees it with eyes overcome by lack and limitation.

For those traveling on the road to empowerment, it is important to know that your power doesn't come from money but from your mind. When you learn how to use this power, you will know how to create a more abundantly lifestyle. This is the power that frees your mind to envision other possibilities. This awakened power in your mind becomes a lightning rod for your actions. You clearly know that you have other options to choose from.

When you empower your mind to envision and search for other possibilities, you change the way you think about how you are presently living. It is the moment when you take the action to understand and love the power you have to change the way you think and live. It is the moment when you stop comparing yourself to other people and accept yourself for who you are. It is the moment when you overcome the weakness of mediocrity.

Many individuals who desire to live life more abundantly are unable to do so because they don't believe they will ever achieve it. It is easier for them to focus on the small, insignificant things in life that lead them to mediocrity and complacency. When you focus on the small things in life such as anger, envy, jealousy, and hatred, you can't see the big picture. A small-minded individual expresses an aura of pettiness in his or her actions. This type of thinking produces a cancerous mind that destroys your will to be successful and live life more abundantly.

Anyone who constantly focuses on the small things in life will find it difficult to believe in empowerment. This lower-level thinking is where victims live, in the shallow parts of the ocean among the reefs of lack and limitation and the barges of worry and fear. For you to overcome victim consciousness, you must train your mind to go farther into the ocean where you will find the limitless thoughts of empowerment.

The goal of anyone who feels restricted by circumstances is to free himself or herself from the restrictions. To change your life, you first must leave the small things behind and swim toward your goal. This means you must empower your mind to stop daydreaming and wishing for something magical to appear in your life. You must know, absolutely, that you are the source of all your actions. There is nothing that can ever happen in your life without your knowing about it.

Today, you have the opportunity to change the way you think and live. To do this requires you to open your mind to see other possibilities. When you free yourself to take this step, you will discover how it feels to live life more abundantly.

The following anecdote will provide you with some information to assist you in your efforts to overcome lack and limitation and learn how to empower your mind to live life more abundantly.

ANECDOTE FOR ACHIEVING ABUNDANCE

The story begins in Peking, China, sometime in 1945. As I walk among the millions of faceless people going hither and yonder, I notice a young man walking toward me with the light of empowerment shining brightly upon his face. His name is Chang. He is a twenty-two-year-old rice farmer who recently moved to Peking to escape the hard times caused by the unexpected deaths of his father and mother.

Since his arrival in Peking, his grief over his parents' death has rendered him powerless to continue managing the 1,000 rice fields they left him. All he can think about now is the loneliness, fear, and lack of self-confidence that cause him to wander aimlessly down the crowded streets searching for the meaning of life.

Today, unlike yesterday, is a bright, sunny day that's good for walking. You can see and feel the beauty in life. For Chang, who stills mourns the deaths of his parents, it is the same as yesterday, another purposeless day to pursue the meaning of life.

Unlike yesterday, today has brought him face to face with his hunger. His body is weak from not having eaten in over two days, although it feels more like two weeks. Chang knows that intense hunger will eventually cause him to lose his perspective on life and succumb to the illusions of starvation.

As he continues to dwell on his hunger and sorrow, he wonders why he came to Peking in the first place. He knows this question doesn't address what's really bothering him, which is not why he's here but what he is going to do about getting something to eat.

Chang watches as throngs of passersby smile and chat with each other. He wants desperately to stop one of them and ask for money. They look so prosperous to him. "Why do other people have so much while I have so little?" he asks himself, while walking aimlessly down the street.

After several hours of walking in the sun, he reaches the point where he knows he cannot continue in this manner. His hunger is driving him crazy, and he must do something quickly to satisfy his hunger and rest his weary body.

Chang continues on his trek with hunger and loneliness guiding him every step of the way. After awhile he stops to rest in front of a crowded café. Perhaps, he thinks to himself, I can ask someone to hire me to work in exchange for some food. Then, as quickly as he thinks about it, he tells himself that as a rice farmer, he doesn't have the skills to work in a large city like Peking. "Who's going to hire someone like me?" he continues to mutter to himself as he greets several of the passersby going into the café.

Chang waits patiently outside the café for over an hour. Overcome with embarrassment, he wipes the sweat from his brow, turns his eyes momentarily from the passersby, and looks upward at the clear blue sky. He stares at the vaporous white clouds, with their monster-like silhouettes prancing across the blue sky. And beneath the clouds, he watches a flock of birds soaring effortlessly to an unknown destination. They continue flying higher and higher until they disappear beyond the clouds.

After several minutes of staring at the sky, Chang feels the hunger pains return. His stomach begins to growl and ache. He turns his back to the street and rubs his stomach to try to soothe the pain.

A few moments later, he peers into the café window just as several people are entering the restaurant. He stares at them while they take their seats and order their food. When the waiter brings their food, he drools and quickly turns away. He suddenly decides to go inside the restaurant and ask the manger for something to eat.

Chang wipes the sweat from his brow again, straightens his clothes, combs his hair, and enters the café to ask the owner for a job in exchange for some food. He asks the waiter to direct him to the owner. The waiter takes him to the owner, who is walking out of the kitchen. Chang approaches the owner, Mr. Teng Li, and says, "Sir, my name is Chang—"

"Chang—Chang what?" Teng interrupts. "Speak up, young one, for I am a very busy man."

"Chang Tse," Chang says, trying to conceal his embarrassment. "I am new to Peking."

"Well, what do you want of me, Mr. Chang?"

"A job. Some food. I am hungry."

"Can you cook?"

"No."

"Are you a waiter?"

"No."

"Well, tell me, Mr. Chang: what can you do?"

"Well, kind sir, I am a rice farmer. That's what I have done all my life."

"So sorry," Teng says. "I don't need a rice farmer. I need a good cook—"

"Excuse me, kind sir," Chang interrupts. "My father and mother died several weeks ago, and I miss them so much. They were all the family I had."

"I am sorry to hear about your loss," Teng says, bowing his head. "As you know by now, the virus has killed many people in China—"

"I know, but I didn't tell you about my parents' death for your sympathy—"

"Then why did you tell me?"

"Because my parents left me 1,000 rice fields to manage. I own them all."

"That's very good, Chang," Teng says, bowing to show his respect.

"Thank you kind, sir," Chang says. "In fact, the rice your customers are eating came from the fields that I own."

"If this is so," Teng says, shrugging his shoulders, "then why don't you have any money to buy yourself some food?"

"Well, kind sir," Chang chuckles, "until two days ago, I didn't have a need for money, because I had so much of it. I also didn't have a need to concern myself with food, because I had so much of it."

"Well, what happened?"

"When I began to grieve over my parents' death, I no longer thought of myself as just a rice farmer. I thought of myself as a man with far greater powers than a rice farmer."

"Oh!"

"I came to Peking not only to escape the loneliness and sorrow caused my parents' death, but to be close to the millions of people who were dependent on me for their food—"

"Uh, pardon me, young man," Teng interrupts. "I don't understand your story. It doesn't make sense to me."

"I know," Chang says, looking up toward the ceiling. "You see, at the time I made the decision to come here, I believed my entire world existed with my parents and the workers of the rice fields. However, something instinctively told me that there was something greater than my power to work in the rice fields. I also knew that I was greater than the 1,000 rice fields that I owned, and the money I earned from them. I knew that I was greater than my needs for money and food."

"I'll say this about you, Chang," Teng whispers, "you have a lot of faith for such a young man."

"Yes, I guess you're right," Chang says. "However, I also have something greater than faith—"

"What is greater than faith?"

"Well, kind sir, when I looked up at the sky, I saw an endless flow of space as the source of food for everyone in the world. The sky did not require money to perform this service. It did so because it has the power to do so.

"That's when I realized that all the power coming from the sky was also coming from me. You see, kind sir, I am a part of the power creating life everywhere in the world, not just in my 1,000 rice fields."

"Okay, let's say I believe you," Teng says, "but what now? I mean, what are you going to do with this newfound knowledge?"

"Well, the first thing I am going to do is accept your kindness and with your permission eat some of the rice produced from my rice fields. After I finish eating, I am going to return to my rice fields, ask one of my workers to bring you payment for my meal, and then continue to supply rice to thousands of people in Peking"

"But—how do you know that I am going to allow you to eat my food without any money?"

"Because I came to you not as a beggar, but as the source of your rice. How can you deny yourself food?"

"I cannot deny myself," Teng says, "but I can deny you—"

"Only if you see yourself separated from me and the rice your customers are eating. What affects me affects you, too. You and I are one with everything that exists on this planet."

"I think I understand you, Chang," Teng chuckles. "You are very wise for your years."

"Thank you, kind sir," Chang says, bowing his head.

"When you really think about it, Chang, I depend on my customers—people whom I have never met until they enter my café—to buy food. Without my customers, I would only have food and a café."

"So true," Chang says. "The millions of people in Peking are a part of you and me, but they don't realize it. Sometimes we all act like strangers to each other."

"Well, Chang," Teng says, "you are quite a special person. You are number one. Come, sit and eat at my table, which is reserved for my special guests. Everyone who works for me knows that whoever sits at this table is a great person. Chang, you are such a person."

"Thank you, kind sir," Chang says. "I will remember your

kindness whenever I look into the face of strangers. You are my reminder that when you become one with one person, you also become one with everyone else in the world."

Chang sits down and begins to feast on a sumptuous meal. He knows the truth about his significance and worthiness to live life more abundantly regardless of his wealth and position.

This anecdote reminds you that you can live life more abundantly without becoming a slave to money and material possessions.

REVIEW OF THE ANECDOTE

1. What emotions did Chang express about the death of his parents?
2. What process did Chang use to overcome intense hunger and gain his confidence?
3. What is the process you currently use to overcome an intense desire for something? Does it work successfully for you?
4. What are the three key emotions that prevent someone from overcoming a serious problem?
5. How would you respond if you felt helpless to overcome something that threatened your life?

Suggestions for Expressing Abundance in All Your Actions

1. Empower your mind to go beyond the struggles to achieve material possessions.
2. Empower your mind to express abundance in all your relationships (personal and career).
3. Empower yourself to see abundance when your senses tell you it is not there.
4. Trust the intuitive-empowerment process to express whatever you desire to see present in your life.
5. Envision yourself living with abundant thinking each moment of the day.
6. Create a new definition of abundance so that you feel comfortable with your life right now.
7. Develop a plan to revalue your life.
8. Create an empowered environment in your home to meditate and pray.
9. Reaffirm your right to achieve success and empowerment.
10. Create a daily action plan to express your vision of living life more abundantly.

Chapter Nine
Power

You and your thoughts are one, but you are greater than your thoughts.

On the road to empowerment, you clearly know that the power that created the universe is greater than the power that created the atomic bomb. Yet the power to create is present in both situations. The power to create anything comes from thoughts like the thoughts you have in your mind. This power is not a stranger, or an alien, or a god separate from you. This power is in your mind.

Whenever you find yourself in a difficult situation or confronted with a seemingly insoluble problem, you automatically think of how to use your mind to solve your problem. To solve a difficult problem, you must think of a new idea. This new idea must not only be vivid in your mind, but it must become a part of your life. Every detail, expression, and action must become a natural part of your behavior. You and the idea must become one, but you must recognize that only you have the power to express the idea.

There are many days when you may feel that you don't possess any power, particularly great power, the type of power that created the universe. Nevertheless, if you are willing to accept that before you were born into this world, you were one in consciousness with the creator of life, then you are able to use your power to overcome any obstacle.

When you become aware of taking your first breath, which confirms your human existence, you know that you are powerful. You are becoming a human being to express the divine purpose of your creator. You know this about yourself because of the covenant you have with your creator. This covenant gives you the right to achieve authentic empowerment and live a successful life during your journey in this world. It does not give you the right to become powerless and accept failure as a way of life. When you do accept that you are powerless and a failure, you become a victim of life's experiences.

A victimized mind is a wasted life that pays homage to the illusions of the world. When you feel like a victim, you act like one. As a victim, you marvel at the power of the illusions expressing themselves as governments, organizations, and economies of the world. These are the powers that weaken your resolve to trust yourself to discover the great powers hidden in your mind.

The search for empowerment or power outside of yourself is an arduous struggle. It becomes an even more difficult search when your mind is overpowered by illusions. A mind overpowered by illusions is a victimized mind, one blinded by dogma and appearances. To search for empowerment, you first must remove the shackles that enslave you to the illusions.

On your journey to achieve enough power to change your life, you must continue to search for it within your mind, which is where your intuitive consciousness is found. This power must not be confused with illusionary powers found in societal positions such as the president of a country or a major corporation.

Whenever you think about achieving power, it means that either you are in an unpleasant situation or you have doubts about your abilities to obtain something that you desire to possess. Regardless of your level of awareness, the desire for power is always present in your consciousness. What you think and know about yourself determines what you think and know about expressing power.

The purpose of changing your life is to assert that you have the power to do it. When you do, you open your mind to see limitless possibilities; however, you must be willing to open your mind. The following anecdote is a tool to assist you with opening your mind to see other possibilities.

ANECDOTE FOR ACHIEVING POWER

There are no mysteries when you discover the great powers buried deep within your mind. You can use this power to travel beyond time constraints by imagining that you are in New Delhi, India, during the summer of 1945, on a hot, humid, teary-eyed day. The sweltering heat, with throngs of people pushing and touching each other, feels like an imaginary hell.

If you look closely at the sunburnt faces of the people walking hurriedly past each other, you can only wonder where they are going as they stop occasionally at one of the shops or street vendors to buy fruit and vegetables.

As you look even closer, you see two pale-faced European men walking hurriedly among the sunburnt faces while trying to escape the sweltering heat, the stench of feces and urine, and the repugnant body odors of the street vendors and beggars.

While maneuvering among the beggars, the men almost trip over a distinctive-looking and rather healthy-looking beggar, who smiles at them with eyes that belie the pain and suffering around him. His face looks like someone used the sun's rays to chisel it with lines of peaceful contentment. And unlike everyone else around him, he doesn't extend his cup for a donation, nor does he seem to be struggling to survive like all the other beggars.

The silence is broken when one of the European men, Nigel Smith, says, "What are you doing here? You seem like you don't belong here"

"You know, Nigel, by god, you're right," says his friend, John Spencer. "This chap is different."

The beggar looks up at them and says, "I am simply a man who chooses to live without human attachments or weaknesses. I am called Amit—"

"Uh, pardon me old, chap, " Nigel interrupts. "My friend and I want to know how you became a beggar."

"I am not a beggar," Amit chuckles. "I have the power to live any way I choose. I choose to live this way because I am proud to say I have held many positions during my lifetimes—"

"What—what do you mean?" John stutters.

"Well, I have lived many lives as a human—"

"You've what—"

"I have lived many lives," Amit says. "During one of my earlier lives, I possessed both wealth and power. I had servants and men who obeyed my every request. Yet I turned away from this lifestyle shortly before leaving my body to pursue the secrets of the universe. That's when I began my search for the answers to life."

"Well, chap, what did you discover?" Nigel asks.

"That I was a prisoner of the illusions that rule this world," Amit says. "Unfortunately, I didn't realize that wealth and power were illusions until I began my journey."

"Then, what—?" John asks.

"I discovered," Amit says, "that all power, illusions and empowerment, comes from a single thought. And if you discipline your thoughts to obey you, you can have everything you want—"

"What—Are you crazy?" John interrupts.

"Yeah, there's something wrong with the chap," Nigel says. "Perhaps the sun has cooked your brains."

The men laugh loudly. "I mean, you have to be crazy to listen to voices inside your head," John chuckles.

"Well, I am not crazy," Amit says. "I am the guardian, the caretaker of my thoughts."

"What are you talking about?" Nigel asks.

"I need to guard against illusions entering my mind to seize my power," Amit says. "If I do, then I have the power to express in the world anything I desire."

"Surely, old chap, you don't believe this, do you?" John says, gesturing with a quizzical expression.

"I not only believe it," Amit chuckles, "I know it. After I died the first time, I found I could remember my previous life even though I was reborn into a different body—"

"What—You don't mean —?" John stutters.

"I do," Amit chuckles. "I reincarnated my thoughts into several different bodies. And each birth allowed me to grow higher in consciousness until I achieved my present level of empowerment."

"Which is what?" Nigel asks.

"That I am greater than the illusions of wealth and power," Amit says. "I am free of material attachments and human limitations."

"But—My God, man, you're a beggar," John says, raising his arms in disgust.

"No, that's what the illusions tell you," Amit says, bowing his head respectfully. "I, and everyone you see here, are greater than what you perceive us to be."

"By golly, old chap, I think you're a little nutty," John says, turning toward Nigel for agreement.

"Yeah, by golly, I think you're right John," Nigel says. "My God, man, everyone knows that true power is with the person who occupies the throne. You know, the queen or king of England. By the way, are you somehow connected to that chap Gandhi?"

"No, but I know him,," Amit says. "I know he seeks to be where I am—"

"What—"

"I mean, at my level of consciousness," Amit chuckles. "Few people ever reach my level of consciousness. For you to reach my level of consciousness, you must conquer the illusions of the world."

"Are you saying that you're greater than the queen?" Nigel asks.

"I am saying that if you reach my level of consciousness, you are free of illusions, which makes you greater than a queen or king."

"I find it difficult to believe you, old chap," John chuckles. "Here you are, a beggar, telling us about true power. If you have so much power, why don't you feed and clothe yourself rather than sitting here begging people for money?"

"Because I am not a beggar," Amit says. "I have everything I need in life to express my purpose for being here. And because I am not dressed like a king, it doesn't mean that my power is not greater."

"Aw, you're a little nuts," Nigel says.

"No, I am not nuts," Amit says. "I am empowered because I sit among the beggars and the merchants and watch the wealthy passersby ignore, scorn, and even despise my existence, and I remain unfazed by their actions."

"What—are you talking about?" John interrupts.

"I know who I am regardless of what I see and hear from others," Amit says. "If I listen to others to tell me who I am, then I will accept that I am a beggar."

"Pardon me, but that's who you are," Nigel says, wiping the sweat from his brow. "Whether you accept it or not, you are a beggar."

"Let me ask you men something," Amit says. "Do you remember who you were before you became aware of yourselves as Nigel and John? Does your queen know?"

"Of course not," Nigel says. "No one knows that. We don't have the power to know. Only God knows."

"But I know," Amit says. "I know who I am now and who I was millions of years ago. I know why I sit here every day and have people provide me with my sustenance. I do so because I provided the world with so much during my other lives. Now it is time for me to receive material sustenance from the world. Even though I receive these gifts, I continue to give what I have to the world."

"But—you don't have anything to give—"

"But I do."

"What?"

"The power to see beyond the illusions in the world," Amit says. "To sit among beggars and thieves and not be either one."

"But—I say you are a beggar—"

"No, I have the power to be among beggars and not be one."

"Only to yourself."

"If this is true, then why did you stop and talk with me?"

"Because you looked different—"

"No, you stopped because my power drew you to me; however, you believed you stopped because you were curious."

"Well, that's true."

"No, ask yourself: Do you believe curiosity motivated you to ask me these questions?"

"Uh—I'm not sure why we've spent so much time with you."

"Perhaps it's because you desire to have my power?" Amit says.

"Well, old chap, you might be right," Nigel says. "I mean, who knows?"

"You do," Amit says.

Nigel and John look at each other befuddled. They stare in silence at Amit, wondering whether he is crazy or not. "It's time for us to bid you farewell, old chap," Nigel says.

"Yeah, old chap, take it easy," John chuckles.

Amit nods his head to acknowledge them and smiles. Nigel and John turn and walk hurriedly toward their destination to escape their confusing interlude with Amit. It's time for them to return to the real world.

Amit watches them turn to walk away and shouts, "You forgot something."

"What?"

"You forgot the gift I have for you."

"Ha, ha, ha, you have a gift for us," Nigel laughs.

"Yes, I have a map for you."

"What kind of map?"

"One that will lead you to the hidden treasure of riches and power."

"Well, old chap, make it fast," Nigel says.

"Yeah," John says, "We've got to go to an important meeting."

"It won't take long," Amit says. "I always give this map as an expression of my love for life to everyone who stops to talk with me."

"Uh, if this map is so important, why don't you give it to one of the beggars around you?" John says. "It seems to me they need it more than we do."

"Perhaps they do," Amit says, "but they have not stopped to talk with me."

"Okay, give it to me," Nigel says.

Amit hands Nigel the map and says, "If you follow the map, it will lead you to your higher power. When you find your higher power, you will know that the beggar and king are illusions."

Nigel looks at the crumpled sheet of paper and sighs.

Amit looks and him and says, "Guard this well, my friend. It is worth more than all the gold in the world."

Nigel thanks Amit as he and John turn and walk quickly down the street, clutching the crumpled map in his hand. They walk briskly away, turning frequently to see whether anyone is following them. They can't wait to take the map back to England and sell it.

REVIEW OF THE ANECDOTE

1. What emotions did Amit express when faced with a challenge to his identity?
2. What process did Amit use to achieve his level of consciousness?
3. What is the process you currently use to maintain your awareness of yourself with power? Does it work successfully for you?
4. What are the three key emotions that prevent someone from expressing the power to overcome what others think about them?
5. How would you respond to someone who labels you as being unworthy to have great power?

Suggestions for Expressing Power in All Your Actions

1. Empower your mind to search for the power that allows you to become a creator.
2. Use the power of intuitive empowerment to change the way you live.
3. Think of yourself as always having the power to achieve your goals.
4. Use your mind to imagine that you have the power to change the way you think, act, work, and live.
5. Empower your mind to go beyond the fears and self-doubts in your life.
6. Honor the power of your mind to create whatever you desire.
7. Create an empowered environment in your home to meditate and pray.
8. Reaffirm your right to achieve success and empowerment.
9. Develop a daily action plan to express your vision of power.
10. Empower your mind to express your ideas in the visible world.

Seeds from the Ashes

Chapter Ten

Creation

When you think like a creator, you refuse to think like a victim.

To truly achieve empowerment, you must commit yourself to overcoming those beliefs that tie you to victim consciousness. This commitment requires you to look beyond the knowledge of the world and deep within your mind for the road map that will guide you to discover what you *really* want to accomplish with your life.

The mind-expansion exercises you have done so far were designed to create a comfort level for you to think beyond your current beliefs. For you or anyone else to change a preconditioned belief, you must be willing to declare its value to your current living conditions. If you believe it works for you, then you will obviously be unwilling to change it. If not, then you are ready to explore some other possibilities.

To think as a creator, you must acquire the power to think with a free, uncluttered mind. When you free your mind of clutter and illusions, you are able to create things similar to or greater than the facsimile machine, computer, airplane, television, wireless phone, and so forth.

When you think as a creator, you trust yourself absolutely. This level of trust implodes as confidence within the essence of your mind. The presence of confidence in your actions empowers you to go beyond your self-imposed limitations. To possess this type of power, you must believe you can attain it.

The ultimate power of creativity is that of the Creator, who created you and the life forms around you. All great people would give anything to have this type of power. The countless unanswered prayers of victims are attempts to gain favor with this power. What if you could have direct access to such power? What would you ask for if you could talk directly to the Creator?

Well, today is the day you stretch yourself to talk directly with the Creator and understand how the Creator exists within your mind. Yes, within your mind is your intuitive consciousness where all things are possible. For you to access this great power, you first must understand what it is. Second, after you understand it, you must be willing to accept it as being a part of your everyday activities. Third, you must use this power to create a new empowered lifestyle.

Whatever you think about your present living conditions, one thing is absolute: You are what you think of yourself. If you don't like your present lifestyle, you have the power to create many different ones. Today, you are strong enough so you don't have to accept mediocrity as your goal. All that is required of you is to know you have all the power you will need to change your life whenever you choose to do so.

To develop your mind to express great power, you must first repair the estranged relationship between your illusions-ridden mind and your freethinking mind. Anyone who has become victimized by the illusions feels powerless to think of himself or herself as being greater than the illusions. The illusions of lack, limitation, and struggle are very powerful when they interfere with your actions to change the way you think and live.

The moment you conquer the illusions in your life, you immediately change the way you act. These new actions reflect a new person. This type of behavior is similar to what some people say is being "born again." And in a certain sense, at least consciously, you are birthing a new person into the world. The new person you are creating will no longer think of himself or herself as a victim of unforeseen circumstances. Once you free your mind of the illusions, you will be able to see clearly where you are going.

When you empower your mind to overcome the barriers that prevent you from living a successful life, you will begin to use your mind to create different outcomes in your life. The next step in the empowerment process is to reaffirm your willingness to accept that this great power is within your consciousness and you can communicate with it anytime you want to.

The following anecdote is a follow-up to an anecdote earlier in the book. It is to help you to examine how you actually feel talking, rather than praying, to the higher consciousness within you.

ANOTHER CONVERSATION WITH YOUR HIGHER CONSCIOUSNESS

"Who calls my name?" the voice says.

"I did," I say. "Are you the last light, Creation?"

"Yes, I am that I am," Creation says. "I am the first and only thought. Everything else exists to express who I am. Every thought in the universe is available for my use."

"Why am I in your presence?" I ask. "Am I here to learn how to become a creator?"

"Yes," Creation says. "I am here to remind you of how to use my power in all your thoughts and desires—"

"But what if I have uncontrolled thoughts and desires?" I ask.

"When you reach me, you know how to discipline your thoughts and desires to obey you," Creation says.

"Yeah, I know," I say. "The other lights taught me how to discipline my thoughts and desires to overcome the illusions. Yet, at some level, I sometimes think I am unable to do this."

"Only when you think you're still a victim," Creation says. "When you free you mind to think like a Creator, you will no longer think of yourself as a victim."

"What do you mean?"

"That you will know the difference between what a victim creates and what an empowered mind creates."

"What's that?"

"The victim mind created the telephone, television, automobile, weapon, and so forth. This lower form of consciousness creates things to serve illusionary desires.'

"Yeah—but some of those creations have served to better our lives as humans."

"Not really," Creation says. "The things you value the most are really worthless to you. For example, the sum total of your medical technology can be summed up in one thought: trial and error to achieve a solution. You have the power to live life without your creations."

"But—"

"You don't know how to use this power."

"That's right. How do you prevent illness or, for that matter, prevent tooth decay?"

"The power to heal your body and mind is in your thoughts," Creation says. "Think about this for a moment: The greatest of all creators, God, the Creator, uses neither science nor medicine to heal or cure what you call diseases."

"I hadn't thought about that," I say.

"All you need to do is discipline your thoughts and desires to overcome the illusions and everything else will be revealed to you."

"Is that all?"

"Yes, there is nothing else."

"It seems so simple. Why can't more people do it?"

"Because they're unwilling to free their consciousness of the illusions," Creation says.

REVIEW OF THE ANECDOTE

1. You are the one conversing with your Creative mind about how to use it to change the way you think and live.
2. Creation is the part of your mind that urges you to use it without fear and reservations.
3. Does the process of communicating with your higher self feel the same as when you are praying to God or another spiritual deity?
4. Do you believe the power to create a new life is present within your mind?
5. Are you willing to use your creative mind to change the way you think and live?

ANECDOTE TO UNDERSTAND CREATION

"Sage, it's really you," I exclaim.

"Yes, Advocate, it is I," Sage says.

"It's really good to see you again."

"It's good to see you again, too," Sage says, embracing me with a fatherly hug. "I am here to help you understand how to think as a Creator."

"Uh, excuse me," I say, interrupting his thoughts. "Do you mean I am going to meet the Creator of all possibilities?"

"Yes, you can say that," Sage chuckles.

"This is what I have longed for all my life," I say. "Now that I have reached this level of consciousness, it seems strange to actually meet the Creator. You know, talk to him like I'm talking to you."

"Believe it or not, you have always talked directly with the Creator," Sage says. "The Creator and I are always present in your intuitive consciousness."

"I didn't realize that until recently," I say. "Before now, whenever I prayed or meditated, I believed the Creator was outside of me."

"Well, that's all behind you," Sage says. "It is time for you to come face to face with the Creator and me. You see, Advocate, the Creator and I are one. When you see the Creator, you also see me—"

"But—if you're the Creator, then who is in my thoughts?"

"I am."

"Have you been with me every step of my journey?"

"Yes, but you didn't recognize me until now."

"That's because I thought the Creator lived outside of my thoughts."

"That's true—"

"Then how does the Creator enter my thoughts, your thoughts, and the thoughts of every life form in the universe?"

"Because every life form is an expression of the Creator's thoughts."

"You mean—"

"Yes, that the Creator's thoughts exist in our thoughts," Sage says. "That's why no other life form can ever kill your higher consciousness. And neither can you kill any other life form. When a life form ceases to exist in the material world, it continues to live in the spiritual world."

"What do they do?" I ask. "I mean, once the body ceases to exist, what happens to the higher consciousness? Does it live in another life form, or does it drift aimlessly in space in a state of nothingness?"

"That's the question you have been seeking an answer to," Sage says. "Those human spirits who rejoin their thoughts with the Creator live differently from those that do not—"

"Uh, excuse me Sage," I interrupt. "What are the differences?"

Sage pauses for a moment and says, "Whenever humans join

their spirits with the Creator while they are in human form, they immediately conquer death by achieving a empowered consciousness."

"What about the others?"

"They replenish the life forms existing throughout the universe."

"That's very powerful," I say. "Even now it's difficult to comprehend and accept that my higher consciousness created this world."

"I know it's difficult to accept this," Sage chuckles. "But if you accept that the Creator actually exists within your intuitive thoughts, then it naturally follows that your intuitive thoughts created this planet. The Creator's power is yours when you know you are one with the Creator—"

"Then why don't I remember creating the world?" I ask.

"You will remember it very shortly," Sage says, assuring me of my success. "Come! Let's travel a little further into intuitive consciousness."

Sage and I travel together to the deepest part of my intuitive consciousness, where my thoughts and his thoughts become one. The further we travel, the clearer my thoughts become of my life with the Creator and the less I remember about my life as a human. It is not long before I begin to see my life and purpose from the Creator's consciousness. In this consciousness, I am everything I desire to be.

"Tell me," the voice says within my thoughts. "Tell me who I am!"

I pause momentarily, because I actually remember the voice. It is the voice of the Creator of all possibilities: a voice I haven't heard since I accepted myself as a human. The joy of just being with the Creator again is exhilarating. I focus my thoughts on the Creator and say, "Creator, is it really you?"

"It is I," the voice says. "I Am that I Am is the one who speaks to you."

My thoughts seem to automatically humble themselves to acknowledge the Creator's presence. I am in the presence of everything that is and everything that is not. There is no life or existence outside the thoughts of the Creator. We are all reflections of this unconditioned consciousness that expresses itself in me as human.

The Creator's thoughts are vast and powerful. Every level of consciousness is complete within itself. The seven lights of empowerment are presence in all the thoughts except one thought: the thought the Creator uses to maintain existence without other life forms.

"Do you remember the moment I allowed you to become human?" the Creator says.

"I do."

"What do you remember?"

"I remember that my existence was without thoughts of beginning or ending. I lived without limitations or desires. I had the power to condition my unconditioned intuitive consciousness to become whatever I wanted it to become."

"Do you remember Sage?"

"I do," I say, continuing to humble my thoughts. "Sage and I have been together since this part of the universe was created. He and I were with you, a part of you, when the Earth and all the stars and planets were created. We have remained a part of the development of life on the planet. I also remember that it was I who asked to come into the world—"

"Do you remember what happened to me?" Sage asks.

"Not until now," I chuckle. "During the time you were guiding me into GAP consciousness and through the seven lights of empowerment, I couldn't remember why you seemed so familiar to me."

"That's why I was with you all the time," Sage chuckles. "You and I are always together, even when we have assumed other life forms. You were with me when I was a human thousands of years ago—"

"Yeah, that's right," I say. "You were called Jesus Christ."

"And you were—"

"The Advocate or Comforter," I say. "The spirit you spoke about to your friends. The one that you were going to ask the Creator to send into the world."

"Right!" Sage says. "I knew it was you that would be coming, because you and I are one."

"That's why you told them I was not greater than you."

"Yes, because all our power comes from the same source, the Creator—"

"Excuse me, Sage," I say. "It wasn't until this moment that I remembered truly why I had entered into the world as a human. Before now, most of my visions were vague and unclear. You know, I had bits and pieces of information about my purpose."

"I know very well, my friend," Sage chuckles. "Only a few humans ever remember their purpose for being in human form. Most of them spend their lives praying to and worshipping an unknown god."

"Yeah, I know," I say, chuckling at the silliness of my earlier exploits. "After you become accustomed to your human body, the memory of your formless, colorless, and faceless self fades away."

"That's why you are in the world now," Sage says.

"For what?

"To remind people to look within their minds for the power to create miracles. As you know, I talked about this power when I was in human form, but I didn't explain it like you and others must do."

"I know."

"Good. It's good that you know the truth about yourself."

"I know."

"The world loves itself," Sage says, refocusing his thoughts on the Creator's presence. "Even though we created the world from a consciousness of absolute power, the possibilities available to humans are limitless."

"I know."

Sage's thoughts express great joy and fulfillment as he focuses on the Creator and me and says, "After you accept yourself as a human, you accept human creations. You learn to rely on things such as language, science, medicine, and mathematics. These human creations become the basis of your existence—"

"Yeah," I say. "That's what happened to your life. Today, people believe you were the Creator's only begotten son, which means no other human can raise their consciousness to the level that you raised yours to."

"I know."

"Strangely, most of the people who think like that don't have a great deal of confidence in themselves." I say.

"I know."

"Fortunately for them, they have the power to change the way they think and live."

"I know,' Sage says. "That's what you and others in the world must remind them of."

"You know, Sage," I chuckle, "sometimes I feel frustrated when I remind people of the great power within them and they look at me like I'm crazy or something."

"It's very difficult for a victim to envision inner power," Sage says.

"Yeah, but it seems easy for them to believe God exists outside of them," I say.

"They think this way because of the illusions that rule the world," Sage says.

"Unfortunately, that's the life of a victim," I say.

"Very good, Advocate," Sage says. "The Creator has empowered you and all others with the seven lights of empowerment to fulfill your purposes as the Advocates for empowerment. As the Advocates, you and the others who dwell in this consciousness will provide the world with insights to empower their minds."

"Thank you," I exclaim. "I now feel more confident about the power I have to change the way I think and live."

"When you do, we shall receive you unto ourselves again," Sage says. "That is the moment when you can truly say that you have conquered the world of illusions. Go and explain those things that I said when I was in human form. Say it so that the others will understand. No riddles, no parables, just what you hear from your higher intuitive consciousness."

"Thank you, Sage," I say. "I love you, Creator. Thank you for my life."

"Go, and fulfill your purpose!"

This anecdote is another exercise for you to measure how far you are willing to go within yourself to discover your higher consciousness. For some people, the thought of talking to your higher consciousness in this manner is not only scary, but also unrealistic.

REVIEW OF THE ANECDOTE

1. You are the Advocate in the exercise. It is you who are advocating the use of empowerment to change the way you think and live.
2. Sage is the wise source of information within you who acts as your guide. He is that part of your consciousness that guides you beyond your illusionary perceptions and limitations.
3. The Creator is the unconditioned consciousness in your mind. This is the ultimate level of awareness where you have limitless possibilities to choose from in your decision-making process.
4. How do you feel knowing that all the power in the universe is within your mind?
5. Are you willing to use this power to change the way you think and live?

Suggestions for Expressing Creativity in All Your Actions

1. Empower your mind to perceive life and power beyond your human awareness.
2. Empower yourself to think that you can achieve great power.
3. Trust the intuitive-empowerment process to express all your ideas.
4. Expand your mind to think about what you desire to express in your life.
5. Think of yourself as a creator or inventor of new things in your life.
6. Affirm to yourself that you are successful and empowered.
7. Discipline your thoughts to focus on your vision of success and empowerment.
8. Affirm your commitment to changing the way you think, act, work, and live.
9. Accept your creative powers as a part of your daily activities.
10. Do the work necessary to express your vision of empowerment in the visible world.

Chapter Eleven
Vision of a New Person

To envision yourself as a new person, you first must stop thinking of yourself as a victim.

The primary reason for you or anyone else to change his or her life is to have a more purpose-fulfilled life. That's why you have read the book up to this point. Now it's time to put some of the information you have learned into a workable, practical, and believable program.

So far, you have learned how to evaluate your life, discover the great power within your mind, and use this power to change your life. The next step in the process is for you to empower your mind to clearly accept that you are changing into a new, more empowered person.

Since you began reading this book and working on changing

your life, I'm confident there are some people who have noticed some changes in your behavior. Even though they may not have told you so, they see the changes. For you, their lack of praise may have affected how you think about the work you are doing to change your life. This is the moment for you to affirm that you are the one who gives value to your work, not someone else.

As you know, the key to transforming your life is your ability to trust yourself. The level of trust you have in yourself depends on the confidence you have in the power of your mind. It is in your mind that you find intuitive consciousness: the consciousness that is able to express all your ideas. The intuitive consciousness houses the seven lights of empowerment, which empower you with clear thoughts and ideas. The lights represent your ability to see clearly without the aid of illusions. Since these are not literally lights, you can define them however you like. For the purpose of assisting you with changing your life, the lights symbolize illumined thoughts that provide form and substance to your ideas.

To successfully use the seven lights, you must attain a high level of self-confidence in your abilities to change your life without assistance from anyone. It is the degree of confidence you have in yourself that gives you the strength to act. When you have any doubts whatsoever about your power, you will experience a roller-coaster journey with overcoming the illusions in your life.

The everyday problems of lack, limitation, and struggle that you face in life are reflections of the confidence you have in yourself.

Vision of a New Person

The greater the problem you face, the greater your confidence must be to overcome it. When you change how you think of the power you possess, you change how you think of your problems. This type of empowered thinking assures you that all problems have solutions.

The chapter on self-discovery prepared you for your journey to change the way you think, act, work, and live. This chapter and the ones that followed it prepared your mind to read the following mind exercise without illusionary restrictions. Now you are in the position to treat this exercise as a tool, rather than a challenge, to provide you with greater clarity about your inner power.

A MIND EXERCISE IN PROBLEM SOLVING.

Let's imagine that you are a married woman with adult children. You have three sisters and one brother, who all have children. Your siblings have prescribed certain behavior traits for you based on their long-term relationships with you. Some of these traits require you to respond to your family members from a position of love and acceptance. This means that no matter what any of the family members do, you are obligated to support them because they are family. And, until recently, you have honored this family tradition.

As with so many families, when your parents passed on, most of your family members discontinued the closeness they enjoyed before your parents died. During the past ten years, some of your family members moved, changed careers, married, divorced, and so forth. It was during this period that your relationships with some of them changed, because they developed closer relationships with other family members than with you.

Some of the family members, including your nephews and nieces, have reacted unfavorably to your new way of interacting with them. They think your new behavior has caused you to dishonor your family ties. A few of them have sought and gained support from your siblings to confirm their beliefs about you.

During the past few years, your family members' actions have had a deleterious impact on you. First, it pains you to finally realize that you had nurtured a dysfunctional family relationship for so long. Second, now that you are aware of this new family problem, you feel compelled to do something about it. Third, you believe that whatever actions you take will only worsen the relationships between you and your family. Fourth, you have been thinking strongly about not having any further relationship with some of your family, including your siblings. Fifth, you wonder whether your new empowerment insights have helped or harmed you. Sixth, since it seems to have happened so fast, you haven't taken the time to understand what happened in the first place.

The truth about others is always the truth about what you think of yourself. The challenge for you to solve this problem is to first understand the factors that caused the problem.

WHAT CAUSED THE PROBLEM?

The problem was caused when you and one of your nieces had a major disagreement over a bank loan. Your niece is a loan officer at the bank where you sought a loan. Since this was the first time the two of you had any business dealings, you thought it was important to share with her the standards you use when you conduct business with large corporations, particularly banks. You also wanted her to know that even though you were family members, you wanted the arrangement with her to be a business one. Your niece agreed.

Your niece explained to you that there would be quite a few documents for you to sign, and since you traveled a lot, she would occasionally fax some of the documents to you for your signature. This would help expedite the loan process.

You agreed with her; however, you made it clear to her that you wanted to personally sign all the documents that require your signature.

Several days later, your niece faxed you several documents to sign, which you signed and faxed back to her. After several weeks, you called your niece to inquire about the status of the loan. She said the loan had been approved and she had the check ready for you to pick up.

On your way to pick up the check, you thought it was strange that the loan had been finalized without your signing the original documents. When you arrived at the bank, your niece handed you the check and duplicate copies of the complete loan documents. As you reviewed the documents, you noticed that the signatures on the final documents were not yours. So you asked your niece what had happened.

She said that she didn't think you would mind her signing your name in order for her to expedite the loan. Moreover, since you all were family, it didn't really matter.

You became upset with her and admonished her for forging your signature. You reminded her of what you had told her earlier about your personally signing all the documents yourself so you would have a clear paper trail.

Your niece couldn't or didn't understand why you were so upset, because all she was trying to do was help you.

You left the office upset, determined to do something about her forging your signature. You thought about going to her supervisor but decided that this might cause her to lose her job. After some contemplation, and because she is your niece, you called her mother and left an urgent voice message for her to call you back. Your sister ignored the message and failed to call you back. Now you were really upset.

You discussed the problem with your husband, who suggested that you call your sister again and try to arrange a meeting with her and your niece. You finally reached your sister, who said she had discussed the matter with her daughter and everything was fine. She said her daughter told her that she discussed the problem with her supervisor, who agreed to call you. Furthermore, her daughter said that she did not want to meet with you because she thought you had disrespected her and she couldn't see how meeting with you would solve anything.

You were hurt by your sister's response and the subsequent call you received from your niece's supervisor. Unfortunately, there was nothing you could do at that point to overcome the problem with her and your niece.

Nearly a year and a half later, you still feel a sense of betrayal by your family. You are still unable to decide what type of relationship you want to have with them. This feeling of betrayal has caused you to question the value of having moral principles if they cause you so much pain and discomfort.

WHAT IS THE EMPOWERED DECISION TO MAKE IN THIS SITUATION?

1. Take the time to relax your thoughts enough for you to know that love is unconditional.
2. Refocus on your empowerment objective.
3. Remove the judgments of right and wrong from your thoughts.
4. Forgive all of those individuals, including yourself, who you believe have caused you to feel the way you do.
5. Contact each family member and explain to them the importance of your honoring the principles and standards

you have chosen to live by.
6. Envision a new relationship between you and the family members.
7. Create clear guidelines to assist you with interacting with your family during this transitional period of consciousness building.
8. Create a clear understanding of your perception of an ideal family relationship.
9. Ensure that all your actions are intended to express the essence of the seven lights of empowerment.
10. Be willing to expand your family base beyond your immediate family.

HOW DOES EMPOWERED BEHAVIOR CREATE A NEW PERSON?

1. When you are able to express forgiveness and love toward those individuals that you believe have caused you pain, you will have made an important step toward achieving authentic empowerment.
2. When you are able to envision clearly what you desire to see expressed in your life, you will create the clarity you need to achieve empowerment.
3. When you are able to express your new values and moral standards to other people without judgment and expectation, you will have gained the strength you need

to trust yourself.
4. When you are able to remove your judgments and opinions about what is right and wrong behavior in others, you will remove these beliefs from your own life.
5. When you take the time to write your moral guidelines on paper, you will enshrine them clearly in your mind and your relationships.
6. When you are able to love strangers as you love your family, you will have achieved the greatness of empowerment.
7. When you are able to express peace in all your actions, you will have attained peace.
8. When you express victim actions toward others, you must be willing to refocus on returning to your empowerment values.
9. When you are unable to perceive some of your actions as being empowered, you must know that every action taken by you is designed to change the way you think, act, work, and live.
10. When you think of someone who is successful and empowered, you think of yourself.

The examination of a problem is the first step in understanding the nature of the problem. The suggestions are insights to stimulate you to think beyond your limitations.

Your ability to perceive yourself today as a more enlightened person than you were several weeks ago is progress. Every change in your activities, no matter how small you might think it is, is a change in the way you think, act, work, and live. Some of the changes you make may appear as innocuous as a single hair on your head, which goes largely unnoticed among the thousands of other hairs on your scalp. Do you fret, worry, and spend a lot of time and energy about losing one hair? Well, you have more thoughts in your head than hairs on your scalp.

There are many times in your life when you feel that one single incident is a life-changing experience. How many times have you said or heard someone else say, "Man, I wish I had made a different decision." "If I hadn't gotten pregnant as a teenager, I could have done so much more with my life." "If I hadn't hung around with the wrong kids, I wouldn't have made some of the decisions I made as a kid."

You can add to the list so many other decisions and actions that have brought you to this place in your life. But no matter how many times you bemoan your past decisions or judge them to have been life-changing experiences, you are still left with the current decision of changing the way you think, act, work, and live. The key word here is *current*.

HOW DO YOU RATE YOURSELF RIGHT NOW?

After envisioning yourself with power and reading this book

Vision of a New Person

and whatever else you have been doing to improve your life, do you think you are presently a very powerful person? What are the attributes you desire to express in your life? Are these attributes consistent with your goal of achieving empowerment?

1. Do you feel that you are better equipped today to solve your problems than you were several months ago?
2. What are the principles that you are using in this moment to change the way you think, act, work, and live?
3. List a significant problem that you have overcome since you began your program to change your life.
4. List five attributes you believe an empowered person should possess.
5. Do you possess these five attributes? If not, why?
6. Do you believe you have chosen the best career to express your greatness?
7. List five things you believe are empowering in the position you currently hold.
8. Do you desire to change careers? If so, why?
9. Do you believe a new career will give you greater power than you currently have now?
10. When you awoke today, did you feel like you had won millions of dollars? If so, describe this feeling. If not, describe how you felt when you awoke today.

WHAT DO YOU THINK OF POOR, INNER-CITY GHETTO FAMILIES?

1. How do you perceive other people that appear to be wasting their lives away?
2. Do you believe poor people can become as empowered as you are right now?
3. Do you believe some people are able to achieve success and empowerment while others are not?
4. List five reasons why you believe people are poor and homeless.
5. List five changes you would like for poor people to make in their lifestyles.
6. Do you feel better or worse off than someone who is poor, homeless, and addicted to drugs and alcohol?
7. List five reasons why you believe you are better or worse off than poor and homeless people with chemical addictions.

WHAT DO YOU THINK OF WEALTHY AND POWERFUL FAMILIES?

1. How do you perceive those people who are rich and famous?
2. Do you believe you are as successful as they are?
3. Do you believe that some people are born special to achieve riches and power?

4. List five reasons you believe people are rich and famous.
5. List five changes you need to make to feel rich and famous.
6. Do you believe the rich and famous are better or worse off than you are right now?
7. List five reasons why you believe you are better or worse off than the rich and famous people.

The exercises are to assist you with evaluating your current understanding of what you think about yourself. The changes you desire to see expressed in your life must be real to you. If you don't believe it, then it isn't so. Regardless of what others say or think about you, you must be committed to changing the way you think and live. It will probably take your spouse, friends, relatives, coworkers, and family members some time to recognize the changes you are making in your life.

Nevertheless, you must be firm in your resolve to trust your inner thoughts to guide you in making decisions. And, as sure as day follows night, your new actions will produce a new person in the world. This new person will have the power to change the way you think and live.

Chapter Twelve
Confirm your Training

The actions you take each day will determine your success.

This chapter provides you with some final insights to use on your journey to change the way you think and live. It is actually a workshop-type approach for you to measure your progress in changing the way you think and live.

The information is outlined in the same format that you would use to participate in an actual workshop. To get the maximum benefits from this information, I suggest that you imagine yourself actually participating in a workshop. This will help you not only to move slowly and thoughtfully through the information, but to conceptualize the importance of completing it. And by completing the material, you will also gain a clear understanding of your current level of awareness.

The truth (awareness) of who you are at any given moment is an important motivational tool to assist you in completing your daily activities. This self-evaluation of your awareness separates illusionary beliefs—those that mislead you into thinking you have overcome a belief—from those that confirm your present awareness. As you know from the work you have done so far, your awareness of power changes from moment to moment. So use this information to guide yourself through those difficult moments when you doubt yourself.

Before you begin the workshop, I suggest that you find a clean, quiet, and comfortable room to work. I also suggest that you complete the material with the fewest interruptions. So it would be ideal to begin after your family members are asleep, away at work and school, or someplace that will not require your presence. The purpose of creating this type of study environment is to simulate your attending a workshop in a hotel or conference center.

SAMPLE WORKSHOP

To begin this workshop, I suggest that you do a ten-minute breathing and meditation exercise. Or you can do the longer version outlined in Chapter One. This will help you to relax your body and mind to focus on expressing the great power in your mind.

The following questions will assist you in evaluating your present level of awareness. They will also assist you in understanding the relationship between your beliefs—what you think about yourself in this moment—and your actions—what you are doing now to change the way you think and live.

PART I - AWARENESS

1. Describe a clear vision of EMPOWERMENT, the goal you have established for yourself. Your vision should be specific about what it is you want to create in your life: for example: wealth, a successful career, happiness in your personal relationships, or the ability to empower your mind to change the way you think and live.

_____
_____
_____
_____
_____
_____
_____

2. Are you presently aware of being the person you envisioned? Yes___, No___. If yes, what evidence do you have to confirm this belief? If no, what actions must you take to become the person you desire to be?

_____
_____
_____
_____
_____
_____
_____

3. Describe how the victim time continuum of past, present, and future time has affected your ability to think, act, work, and live successfully in the present moment.

_____
_____
_____
_____
_____
_____
_____

PART II - BELIEFS

1. Define five key beliefs that are in your inner or intuitive consciousness.

_____
_____
_____
_____
_____
_____
_____

2. Define five key beliefs that are in your victim consciousness.

_____
_____
_____
_____
_____
_____
_____
_____

3. Describe the process you used to identify your intuitive and victim beliefs: (Categorize and list each belief with the appropriate process used).

_____
_____
_____
_____
_____
_____
_____
_____

PART III - ILLUSIONS

1. Describe five illusions (problems) that you have faced since the initial conception of your vision of empowerment and the work you are doing to express it in the world.

_____

_____

_____

_____

_____

_____

_____

2. Describe the appearance (form and image) of each illusion and rank its importance in impeding your progress to change the way you think and live. (List each illusion separately.)

_____

_____

_____

_____

_____

_____

_____

3. Describe the circumstances that allowed these illusions (problems) to enter your life. For example: How were you feeling at that time? Did they stop you from working on your vision? (List and describe the illusions in the same order as for question 2.)

_____
_____
_____
_____
_____
_____
_____
_____

PART IV - ACTIONS

1. Describe the specific actions you took when you confronted the five illusions listed in question 2 above. List each illusion in the same order as above.

_____
_____
_____
_____
_____
_____
_____

2. Assign each of the actions above to either the intuitive consciousness or the victim consciousness category.

_____
_____
_____
_____
_____
_____
_____
_____

3. Describe your level of self-confidence in taking intuitive action to solve the problems listed above. List each problem separately.

_____

_____

_____

_____

_____

_____

_____

PART V — PROBLEM SOLVING

1. Describe a difficult problem that you are currently working on.

2. Describe the origin of the problem and the circumstances that brought it into your life.

3. How did this problem achieve such great importance in your life?

4. List the first steps you need to take to solve this problem.

5. Describe how these actions are consistent with your original vision of empowerment.

_____
_____
_____
_____
_____
_____
_____

6. Describe why you believe these actions are powerful enough to solve your problem.

_____
_____
_____
_____
_____
_____
_____
_____

SELF-EMPOWERMENT PROCESS

1. **CONCEPTION** (the idea) IS GREATER THAN ITS **EXPRESSION** (what you have created).

2. **FOUR STEPS TO EMPOWERMENT**
(Refer to Chapter Five)
   1. VISION OF EMPOWERMENT.
   2. EMBODIMENT OF THE VISION.
   3. ACCEPTANCE OF THE CREATIVE PROCESS.
   4. DAILY ACTIONS TO EXPRESS THE VISION.

CAUSE AND EFFECT

PAST	PRESENT	FUTURE
I should have…	I am…	I will be…
I wish I had…	I am…	I hope to…
If I hadn't done…	I am…	I will be…

VICTIM	EXTERNAL ISSUES	NEW SELF
POWERLESS	STATUS/TITLE	SUCCESS
LACK	RESOURCES, MONEY	SUCCESS
LIMITATION	UNABLE TO ACHIEVE	SUCCESS
STRUGGLE	DAILY PROBLEMS	SUCCESS
DOUBT	DISTRUST ABILITY	SUCCESS

Chapter Thirteen

Vision of a New Family

The vision of a new family comes from an empowered mind.

The end of this book is actually the beginning of a new life for the reader. Since you have taken the time to read the book, I must also take the time to write this chapter in a way that stimulates you to act. This chapter is a way for you to expand the limits of your mind to pursue things yet to come. It is an opportunity for you to focus on empowerment solutions for yourself and countless families in this country and around the world.

The true meaning of changing your life is expressed in the interactions you have with your family. For an individual to change the way he or she thinks and lives is not enough unless this information is shared with others. The collective human actions are what build neighborhoods, cities, and countries. In other words, for you to become empowered and ignore the plight of others who are victimized by the illusions of the world is an affront to empowerment. While empowered change begins and ends with the individual, the true essence of empowerment is found in the footsteps of the victims of illusions, who ignore its presence.

Several weeks ago, I became a little concerned when I discovered that I lived in a rapidly changing, technologically challenging society. It all began innocently enough with my shopping for a software package to help me track my clients and identify business opportunities. Simple enough, right? No, it's an experience I won't forget anytime soon, because I had to consider some options that required me to change my reliance on Rolodexes, cards, and other so-called outdated things.

I was introduced to some gadgets such as Flash Drive (a mini disk, the size of a small highlighter, that stores information like a compact disk) and an electronic organizer in which I can store everything I used to have in my appointment book. Basically, these gadgets freed me of paper. They also made me face the possibility of giving up my comfort level of using appointment books, Rolodexes, and business cards.

I didn't feel good about having to change my habits, so I held on as long as I could to my old habits while I reluctantly transitioned to the new ones. It wasn't long before I realized that I couldn't use both of them without duplicating my work. I chose the new gadgets.

I am sharing this experience with you to let you know how we fight to hold on to those things that we are comfortable with. Every belief that we have is dear to us. We hold on to them without ever realizing that there are greater opportunities awaiting us if we would only let go of those beliefs that are stifling our empowerment growth. How often do you or someone you know quote a parent or grandparent about morality and values? "My mother told me…." We frequently rely on information from people that we love and trust. This doesn't mean it is valid or current information. It only means this is what you were taught and you have accepted it as part of your beliefs.

How many of you would go to your parents or grandparents to ask them how to install a Flash Drive in your computer? I suspect it would be a small number of people who would seek technological information from their parents. The same is true for empowerment and moral principles. If you want to know something different about how to live, you have get it from the new *you*. Old-thinking individuals seldom develop new things.

When you take the time to compare the technological advances in the world with the spiritual advances, you quickly discover a wide disparity between the two. While technology has moved forward drastically in the past twenty years alone, spirituality and morality have remained basically the same in this country since the seventeenth-century adoption of the King James Bible.

Most people are afraid to examine or explore ideas that are not contained in one of the Holy books. If you mention the moral and spiritual decadence that is destroying the lives of millions of Americans, you are referred to the Ten Commandments for the answers. These same individuals frequently lament, "If only people would obey the Ten Commandments, the world would be just fine." Perhaps, but significant numbers of people are not obeying them.

It seems to me that people believe God talks only to certain people, such as the ones who are inventing the technology today. Apparently, he told only the early writers how people should live for future generations. Is this why we accept the ideas of the dead and scorn those from the living?

It seems strange for technologically dependent individuals to believe someone was divinely ordained to write brilliant spiritual prose that never envisioned an airplane, fax machine, computer, or automobile, not to mention things such as cellular phones, compact disks, iPods, and so forth.

There are many individuals in this world who have received genuine insights from the Creator, but for unknown reasons, possibly fears, they have not been heard by the masses. Perhaps you are one of those people. If you are, you must use your great power of mind to create something new in the world.

For the purpose of empowerment training, you can use the tools in this book to perform a creative exercise to create a new family. Your new family does not currently exist—you must create it by using the morals and values expressed in the seven lights of empowerment. The goal for the new family is to create the structure that will empower inner-city families to overcome the psychological and cultural problems destroying the neighborhoods.

Most of the psychological and cultural decay has its greatest impact on African and Latin Americans. Yet the family model you are creating will also empower other individuals who feel powerless to change their lives. In far too many instances, obsequious thoughts by powerless-thinking individuals are responsible for creating ghettos. The new family model you are creating must overcome these limitations.

I said in the introduction to this book that I kept seeing visions of people living hopeless lives in cities and towns throughout the country. I saw these images become realities during the Katrina hurricane and its mass destruction of property and the lives of thousands of people in New Orleans and Mississippi. It was painful to watch so many powerless people struggling to live in an alien society without the proper tools.

Some of the concerns expressed by those watching the experience on television confirm what most people think about the status of inner-city blacks: They are unable to take care of themselves without government assistance.

Most African Americans—or blacks, Negroes, coloreds, or whatever makes you comfortable to say—have survived in this country without strong family morals and values. This lack of a strong family has had a deleterious effect on their ability to create strong, self-sufficient neighborhoods. Sure, the blame can be laid on the doorstep of slavery and its policies of separating family members from each other for economic gain. But this is not the true reason for the degeneration of the black family. The real culprit is a lack of moral principles and values that empower people who were deprived by society from creating an empowered family structure.

From my research and work with inner-city blacks, I believe the absence of a strong, workable family structure in the ghettos of America has had a deleterious effect on the social, economic, political, and religious development of racial minorities. And to make matters even worse, the current acceptance by many young black men and women of a social morass that gives power to procreation and violence have created a generation of social, economic, political, and religious eunuchs. These actions and those of past generations have radically trivialized the power blacks have to transform their lives. Unfortunately, this trivialization of power has created generations of powerless individuals who depend on someone (God, the government, or a leader) to solve what they generally accept as insoluble problems.

Many of the major problems faced by the racial minorities, including problems of racism, poverty, violence, addictions, diet, self-hatred, single-family heads of households, and a preoccupation with and focus on using entertainment and sports to achieve power are individual problems. This means that each individual must first overcome the deleterious effects created by these problems.

The victimized mind is unable to free itself from the effects of powerlessness. To overcome victim beliefs, you must first overcome the beliefs that cause you to think you are a victim and live a victim's lifestyle. This means that everyone living in a neighborhood must first empower their minds to think and live beyond the self-imposed victim beliefs of lack, limitation, and struggle. It also means that one person can begin this process of empowerment. That one person's actions will have an immediate impact on his or her family members, which will have an impact on those who interact with each of the family members.

While all change begins with an individual, change takes on a greater meaning and significance when it involves other people, particularly other people who seek to change the way they think and live. The whole purpose of changing your life is for you to interact with others with an empowered mind.

There are many inner-city individuals who believe individual success is all that is necessary for someone to have a successful life. They believe this because blacks were taught to function outside of a formalized family structure and minimize the importance of an empowered nuclear family.

To overcome these types of victim beliefs, you must first

understand their importance to blacks in surviving slavery, segregation, integration, and assimilation. Many black communities were held together by the spoken words of right and wrong passed from generation to generation. There was a considerable amount of time devoted to learning how to survive with a modicum of success and dignity in a truly racially segregated society. Few blacks were bold enough to raise questions about the way they lived. Most of them just wanted to get ahead by having nice clothes, cars, houses, and so forth. Unfortunately, these are the beliefs and actions that created the people in New Orleans who represent a microcosm of poor, inner-city blacks throughout the country.

The challenge before you and me is how to use the power we have to change the way we think, act, work, and live. Obviously, there is no right or wrong answer or anyone who can tell us what to do. It is a challenge of the individual mind to express the power it has to enlighten the minds of everyone you come in contact with.

Today, I hear the silent voices (ideas) pushing themselves to the forefront of my mind. They speak, I listen, and then I act. The purpose of using this book as a guide to creating a new way to think, act, work, and live is, without question, a clear one.

For you to change or create something new, you must boldly take the first step. The first step in creating a new inner-city family is to adopt some principles that will empower you to live an empowered lifestyle. So, to begin the process, I am proposing a new set of principles to rebuild the inner-city family.

Empowerment Solutions for Creating Family Values

1. I acknowledge the presence and power of the Creator within me.
2. I acknowledge that everyone is empowered by the Creator.
3. I acknowledge that it is my inherent right to create and express empowered images of myself.
4. I acknowledge that I have the power within my thoughts to change my life.
5. I acknowledge that I have the power to create success and empowerment in all aspects of my life.
6. I acknowledge that I have the power to express love, peace, wisdom, freedom, abundance, power, and creation in all of my actions.
7. I acknowledge that I have the power to live my life without being victimized by lack, limitation, and struggle.
8. I acknowledge that I have the power to live free of all forms of addictions and illness.
9. I acknowledge that I am empowered to create a successful and prosperous environment for my family.
10. I acknowledge that all my power comes from the Creator of all possibilities.

I am sharing the ten principles outlined here to challenge you to think about the limitless possibilities available to everyone who dares to seek empowerment. There is nothing magical about them. You will not change your life by reciting them as a mantra. These principles will work only after you do the work to free your mind to unleash the great power hidden within your consciousness.

I am going to share with you the meaning of each of the ten principles. As you grow in empowerment, I am confident you will create new ones.

Principle One:

I acknowledge the presence and power of the Creator within me.

To acknowledge the presence and power of the Creator within you requires an awareness beyond the limitations of what you have been taught by others. It requires that you know with certainty that you and the Creator are one, but the Creator is greater than you. The conception (intuitive consciousness) is greater than that being created (you and your limitations). In other words, the Creator is in you, not in the sky.

Principle Two:

I acknowledge that everyone is empowered by the Creator.

To acknowledge that everyone is empowered by the Creator requires you to have the awareness that you (intuitive consciousness) are also present in all humans. This awareness frees you of societal descriptions of people based on skin color, gender, religion, status, and wealth. You free yourself to think and create from a position of power without limitations.

Principle Three:

I acknowledge that it is my inherent right to create and express empowered images of myself.

The power to change yourself is expressed in your abilities to imagine you are different from what you heretofore believed about yourself. For example, if you believe you are deficient in the area of education, you will present yourself as being educationally deficient to others. After awhile, this become the image you have of yourself. To change this image only requires you to change the way you think of yourself.

Principle Four:

I acknowledge that I have the power within my thoughts to change my life.

What you think is who you are. No matter how much you desire to change your life, you cannot do it without changing the way you think about yourself. A single thought can change your life if it is conceived from your higher intuitive consciousness.

Principle Five:

I acknowledge that I have the power to create success and empowerment in all aspects of my life.

The successful person is the one who believes and acts successful. The empowered person is the one who has discovered the great power of intuitive consciousness. You stand at the door of your consciousness where these two powerful thoughts exist. Knock hard, and the door will open and they will become one with your thoughts.

Principle Six:

I acknowledge that I have the power to express love, peace, wisdom, freedom, abundance, power, and creation in all of my actions.

The seven lights of empowerment are always within your intuitive consciousness. The choice to use them is always yours. No matter what you think of yourself today, you can become a master of these great lights of empowerment. Look for them in the hidden regions of your mind.

Principle Seven:

I acknowledge that I have the power to live my life without being victimized by lack, limitation, and struggle.

The idea that you lack the power to express the images you create of yourself is pure folly. Every day you express what you think of yourself. Only self-inflicted wounds of doubts create the limitations on your power to express new ideas. Remove your doubts and watch your limitations disappear. A victimized mind besieged with low self-esteem and low self-confidence struggles to achieve goals set by other people. After awhile, the idea of struggling to achieve success becomes a way of life. Remember: There's no struggle in creation because it's an effortless process.

Principle Eight:

I acknowledge that I have the power to live free of all forms of addictions and illness.

When you succumb to addictive behavior of drinking alcohol, using drugs, and overeating, you lose your power to achieve empowerment. Only the person who has overcome the desire for chemicals as a panacea for his or her problems will taste the fruits of empowerment. The power to cure all illness is contained within your intuitive consciousness. Heal yourself by empowering yourself.

Principle Nine:

I acknowledge that I am empowered to create a successful and prosperous environment for my family.

The empowered person expresses power in all aspects of his or her life. The nuclear family unit is presented with a clear awareness about beliefs of spirituality, morality, values, education, community interaction, and economics. Children are taught the meaning of the seven lights of empowerment throughout their developmental years. Parents continue to focus on developing their minds to achieve a clear awareness of their purposes.

Principle Ten:

I acknowledge that all my power comes from the Creator of all possibilities.

There is only one power in the universe, and that power is within the consciousness of the Creator of all possibilities. The powers that humans have over each other is not really power, but the illusion of power. The power that you have over all your thoughts is real power. If you can rise beyond your awareness of yourself as someone consumed by illusions, then you will transform yourself from a powerless person to an empowered one.

These ten principles are basically a guide for you to use as you travel on the road to empowerment. They stimulate your thoughts to action. This will allow you to expand your knowledge base to include information you were heretofore afraid to confront. The empowered person goes hither and yonder, interacting with all types of people. He or she is present in each person's actions, but not a part of the knowledge used to express the actions.

Empowerment allows you to be in the presence of murderers, thieves, alcoholics, drug addicts, and prostitutes without judgment or desires. You travel many roads, but no road holds the complete truth about who you are. Only you know the answer to that question.

The final mind-expansion exercise is designed to incorporate the seven lights of empowerment into the concept of a new inner-city family. This new family is created to address the current issues facing inner-city African and Latin American families, as well as European, Asian, and Native American families.

The scenario that is used to describe the new family is not the only one that can be effectively used. There are many individuals who currently live in family situations that exclude both parents. The new family recognizes and accepts that the ideal family is an empowered one: a family that has embodied the new principles of empowerment. This means that an unmarried woman, with children can become a model family within the new neighborhood even though many victims will continue to perceive her and her family as being unworthy to symbolize an acceptable family model.

Nevertheless, she and her children can be considered an acceptable family model because of their embodiment of the empowerment principles. No one is penalized or ostracized from the neighborhood because they do not meet the ultimate objective of having both parents in the model family structure.

Similarly, the vision we are using to create a new family model is a mind exercise for those who are familiar with the seven lights of empowerment. The vision is a cumulative expression of the steps that you have used so far to change the way you think, act, work, and live. This means that everything we use to create the new family must include the seven lights of empowerment.

VISION OF A NEW INNER-CITY FAMILY

Now, in the final moments of the book, I see a vision of a new inner-city family: the family that I kept in my thoughts throughout the book. This family is empowered and lives in the present time in a city in the United States of America.

The family structure consists of a man, a woman, and four children, two boys and two girls, ages 7, 13, 10, and 16, respectively. The man and woman have been married for eighteen years. They were born into a traditional Christian family. The father was raised as a Baptist and the mother as a Pentecostal. Both parents are high school graduates with some college. The father is a former gang member and drug addict, while the mother never smoked or drank. They both are seekers of empowerment.

On a hot summer night, they come face to face with a crisis of faith when their house is sprayed with bullets during a drive-by shooting between warring gang members. When the carnage is over, the family raise their heads to survey the damage caused by nearly a hundred gunshots. The parents can only stare at the horror before them. As they continue to survey the house and ensure that everyone is okay, they discover the mortally wounded, lifeless body of their seven-year-old son lying in a pool of blood amidst the broken glass.

The father bends down to check his son's pulse only to discover that he doesn't have one. He cries loudly with sounds that can be heard by all who have tasted death among a loved one. His shocked family embraces him with hugs and tears while searching for words to express their grief. They quickly realize there are no words to describe the pain you feel when someone you love dies. So they remain in a death-like moment with only the whispered sobs and gasps that come from deep pain and grief.

The family buries their son several days later. All that most of them remember is that they don't remember anything about the funeral. During the days and weeks after the funeral, the parents search for ways to move beyond the deep pain and anger eating away at them. Whom can they blame? Who's responsible?

A couple of months after the funeral, the father says he blames God for allowing their son to die such a horrible death. The mother, at first, is reluctant to blame God. It will take her two more weeks to agree with her husband that God was responsible for their son's death.

Now that they have found someone to blame, it seems easier for them to move on. Although time is moving forward, anger continues to rule their lives. With both of them consumed by anger, they pledge to never attend church again, nor will they pray to or worship God.

The father begins to drink heavily and spend long hours away from home. Shortly afterwards, the mother begins to drink heavily, too. With both parents consumed by alcohol and anger, the children are neglected. The oldest girl also begins to drink, smoke weed, and have sex with boys. The older boy decides to immerse himself in books, while the youngest girl stops talking altogether. The once proud and united family is falling apart.

One day, while nursing a hangover and standing in front of a window, with the sunlight shining directly on his face, the father turns away momentarily toward the large mirror several feet behind him. As he stares into the mirror, he is temporarily blinded by the bright sunlight shining through the open window. He closes his eyes for a few moments to help him see. When he opens his eyes, he looks into the mirror and sees the face of a strange man. He asks himself, "Who is the stranger in the mirror?" The response is deafening silence.

He watches the man's hands write messages on the mirror; however, as he turns away to look at his own hands, he notices they aren't moving at all. With a startled expression, he turns to stare into the mirror for clues about what's happening to him. He stares into the mirror, and once again the strange man is scribbling messages on the mirror.

A couple of minutes later, he is able to read the messages on the mirror. They instruct him to move forward with his life and let go of the anger that is killing him. He must forgive those who killed his son; until he does, he will be unable to move forward with his life.

Several moments later, the stranger is gone, and so is his message on the mirror. All that is left on the mirror is the image of a downtrodden, angry man staring blankly into it. "What kind of trick is this?" he asks himself as he quickly turns away from the mirror.

A few seconds later, he turns back and looks into the mirror again. This time he notices that the image of himself has changed into that of another stranger. The image before him now is that of an empowered man whose face is free of fear, worry, and anger. The image begins to write on the mirror about how to move beyond the pain and grief. It is a simple and clear message about how he can create a new family. It says that he should use the seven lights of empowerment—love, peace, wisdom, freedom, power, abundance, and creation—to build his new family.

He is overwhelmed with joy as he turns from the mirror and kneels down to pray for the first time in a long time. He hears the voice of the Creator tell him to search for the door within him that unlocks the secrets of empowerment. Behind the door is everything he needs to create a new family. He feels the presence of the Creator in his mind. He wants to believe it is actually the Creator, but he is unsure. He's too afraid to trust himself.

He rises from the floor feeling like a load has been lifted from him. He clearly knows what he has to do to bring his family together again. The first thing he has to do is to immediately stop drinking alcohol. Then he quickly rushes to his wife and tells her about the vision in the mirror. He explains to her how God revealed to him how to create a new family and how he needs her support with this project. However, she first must agree to stop drinking. She agrees to stop drinking and to do whatever she can to assist him with creating a new family.

He hugs her and says, "All I know is that a few days ago I was angry about the death of my son. So angry that I blamed God for his death without ever realizing his death was caused by some neighborhood gang members."

The father and mother stop drinking for several months. During this time they begin to meditate and pray for the power to understand how to build this new family. After several months of soul searching for answers, the father is standing once again in front of the window looking out at the trees and birds, with the sunlight beaming down on the mirror several feet behind him.

This time, he turns around quickly to look into the mirror. As he does so, the sunlight shines directly from the mirror into his eyes, which blinds him for a few seconds. He rubs his eyes and opens them to look directly at the silhouette in the mirror. As he clears his eyes, the silhouette looks more and more like him. He looks closely into his face and notices seven lights shining from his eyes. Each light has a label that corresponds to the seven lights of empowerment that he was told to search for within himself.

He watches as each light writes messages on the mirror. When they are finished, he has the Ten Principles of Empowerment that he can use to build a new family. As he looks closer, he sees the instructions on how to use each principle. He now has all that he needs to build a new family.

He shares the principles with his wife and explains to her the instructions he received from the seven lights of empowerment. She is somewhat skeptical about the lights writing on the mirror, but she goes along with her husband because of all the progress he has made in changing his life, particularly his abstinence from alcohol They adopt the principles in their daily activities and begin to teach their children how to use them.

In the process of teaching the children, they create ten

principles especially for them:

Ten Principles of Empowerment for Children
1. Teach each child from the beginning how to discipline his or her thoughts.
2. Teach each child from the beginning how to understand his or her actions.
3. Teach each child from the beginning to have faith in their parents to teach them the truth about achieving and expressing empowerment.
4. Teach each child from the beginning how to have faith and confidence in their abilities to express success and empowerment.
5. Teach each child from the beginning how to distinguish between the real and unreal expressions of the illusions of the world.
6. Teach each child from the beginning how to live free of resentment in the face of persecution.
7. Teach each child from the beginning how to understand and use the seven lights of empowerment (love, peace, wisdom, freedom, abundance, power, and creation).
8. Teach each child from the beginning how to form a vision of empowerment.
9. Teach each child from the beginning how to have devotion of purpose to the vision of empowerment.

10. Teach each child from the beginning how to live free of all addictions.

The eldest daughter is reluctant to accept the ten principles. It takes her awhile to believe that the principles can assist her with addressing the pain in her life. She finally agrees.

Everyone in the neighborhood begins to notice the change in the family's behavior. It is as if they have been reborn as new people. Some of the men and women stop by their house to inquire about how they were able to change their lives.

The man and woman freely share the information. It seems that the more information they give to the community, the more people want more information. After awhile, the family decides to create an Empowerment Center where everyone in the neighborhood can come and exchange information about the twenty principles of empowerment.

CONCEPT OF AN EMPOWERMENT CENTER

The concept of an Empowerment Center where families own and operate the facility is readily received by most of the people in the neighborhood. They agree to model the center after the seven lights of empowerment and the twenty principles of empowerment. The enlightened ones create the cornerstone of consciousness from which the center will be built.

1. Each family who completes the empowerment training will

invest an equal share of money to build the center.
2. Each family who completes the empowerment training will invest a stipulated amount of money each month for the maintenance of the center.
3. The center will designate seven rooms of equal size to use to teach the seven lights of empowerment (love, peace, wisdom, freedom, abundance, power, and creation).
4. The center will designate a large room to use as a cafeteria to serve chemical-free food and drinks.
5. The center will designate several rooms for meditation training.
6. The center will designate rooms to teach each family how to produce income to provide for their own individual family, as well as to create businesses and jobs to employ everyone in the neighborhood.
7. The center will commit to working with individuals to empower neighborhoods around the world.

When the training is completed, the neighborhood will become a beacon of empowerment for everyone to see and use. There will be no crime, unemployment, underemployment, use of alcohol or drugs, or abuse toward women and children. New businesses that enhance the empowerment growth of the neighborhood will spring up everywhere. The businesses will hire people from within and outside the neighborhood; however, no one will be hired until they complete the empowerment-training program at the center.

The power to change your life comes from within you, not from money and other people. The new family is one drastically different from the images we see of inner-city families in cities and towns throughout the country. The new family is empowered and able to take care of itself, because it recognizes that all power is contained within your mind.

The new family is a simple concept. The challenge is for individuals to accept that change is possible right now.

ABOUT THE AUTHOR

Malcolm Kelly is a Social Philosopher. He is president of MKA Consulting Services and the National BYE Society.

Malcolm currently conducts *empowerment solutions*™ seminars that provide individuals with the tools to change the way they think and live. He serves as a keynote speaker for diverse business, educational, and social organizations throughout the country.

As a writer, his cutting-edge articles have appeared in many major newspapers, and his books have provided readers with bold, thought-provoking ideas to assist them with changing their lives. His work with inner-city families has made him a leading advocate for teaching individuals social responsibility and the importance of using your inner power to solve your problems.

His civic and business experience include serving as chairman of the Oakland Civil Services Commission, a director of the Bay Area Urban League, president of the Alameda County Industry Education Council, a successful business owner, and the founder of the National BYE Society.

Malcolm has a M.A. degree in Philosophy and has taught classes on the African-American Family. He is the author of the highly acclaimed books *The New African American Man* and *Let There Be Life*.

www.ingramcontent.com/pod-product-compliance
Lightning Source LLC
Chambersburg PA
CBHW071659090426
42738CB00009B/1592